ADVENTURES IN
MANIFESTING

ADVENTURES IN MANIFESTING

LOVE AND ONENESS

Sarah Prout and Sean Patrick Simpson

The Adventures In Manifesting series: Volume #5.
First published 2012 by Älska Publishing

Office based in Melbourne, Australia

Typeset in Giovanni LT 9/12/14 pt

© Sarah Prout and Sean Patrick Simpson

The moral rights of the authors have been asserted.

National Library of Australia Cataloguing-in-Publishing entry:

Authors:	Prout, Sarah 1979 – / Simpson, Sean Patrick 1984 –
Title:	Adventures In Manifesting: Love and Oneness
ISBN:	9780987325914 (pbk) 9780987325952 (ebook)
Subjects:	Self help, New Age Publications, Inspiration
Dewey Number:	152.41

Cover design by Sarah Prout

Editorial revisions in house

Printed in Hong Kong

Also available in electronic format

*note that grammar and US/UK English is sometimes reflected in each author's preferred writing style.

www.AlskaPublishing.com

Wholesale Discounts
For competitive rates on bulk purchases, please go to www.AlskaPublishing.com

Disclaimer
The material in this publication is of the nature of general comment only and does not represent professional advice. To the maximum extent permitted by the law, the authors and publisher disclaim all responsibility and liability to any person, arising directly or indirectly from any person taking or not taking action based upon the information in this publication.

Älska means to LOVE
(Say it like this: *elsh-ka*)

This book is lovingly dedicated to Oprah Winfrey.

CONTENTS

Conclusions

GRATITUDE

With the deepest gratitude we would like to thank all of the Älska authors for sharing their incredible and inspiring stories in this book. We would also like to thank our students in the **AdventuresInManifesting.org** community and *you* (the reader) for supporting the Älska vision of Love and Oneness.

From Sean:

The creation of the latest three Adventures in Manifesting books have been an absolutely incredible and inspiring process. My deepest gratitude is with our project manager Mark Rhapsody for all he has done.

To Sarah Prout – you are amazing and I love you. It is such a joy waking up to you each morning and spending our days playing in the fields of Älska Publishing. Living in the now, reminiscing on the past and dreaming about the future with you is amazing.

To Amr and Angel – thank you for your incredible work. To Olivia and Thomas who are a constant reminder *to be the change*. S&D – You're always to be thanked. To Mom and Dad, you guys rock. To my crew, who are always in my heart every single day.

To some of my greatest inspirations I have yet to meet and befriend: Oprah, Ellen, Will Smith, Jim Carrey, and Richard Branson. Thank you for *being* and inspiring the world not just through what you do, but by who you are.

To everyone in my life, my deepest love and gratitude is with you.

From Sarah:

I would like to thank my dad (Mr. A.A Prout) for your love and support. Your kindness and help with the kids is so greatly appreciated – I love you.

To my man, Mr. Sean Patrick Simpson – you're my best friend and I adore you. Your sublime management skills and dedication to the rapid growth of our company and vision is a true inspiration.

Thomas and Olivia, I love you with all my heart. Thank you for being the beautiful souls that you are.

To my friends, family, and soul family (you know who you are) – thanks for your amazing love and support. It means the world to me.

Many thanks to our awesome team behind the scenes here at Älska-Publishing that keep the company running like a well-oiled machine.

Last but not least… our fur babies Cookie LaLa and Merlin Moon-man – you really are amazing little souls in dog suits.

INTRODUCTION

Älska

It is with soul-felt gratitude that we would like to welcome you to the *Adventures in Manifesting* series. It has been designed as a source you will continuously enjoy reading when in search of insight, wisdom, and inspiration. The stories are shared from people just like you that are on a wondrous journey of self-discovery.

From a multitude of unique vantage points, these stories demonstrate active examples of inner guidance, connection, faith, and love that have transcended all limitations. Each story has been written with you in mind.

Reading with Your Soul

Our advice to you is that you read with an open heart, an open mind, and absorb the information that sparks your own adventure in manifesting. When reading from a place of wonderment and curiosity, you are bound to find deep resonance. Ask yourself, "What here resonates with me? What inspired action am I being guided to take? What can I learn from this now?"

Allow yourself to find a connection point within each story and within yourself that is right for you.

Your Own Treasure Map

While you will discover truths that each author has found for themselves, you can find in-between the lines your own truths as well. The wonder of this book is that understanding and resonating with certain concepts will happen at different points in your life. So take your time. Keep the book by your bedside table. Pick it up when you feel inspired and follow your inner guidance to the story you're meant to draw from now. Whether you read through it all in one sitting, or piece-by-piece, you will find this a place of inspiration for years to come.

The Mission of Älska

The mission of Älska is to bestow the teachings of love and oneness and proliferate its message throughout the world. Within these two illuminated concepts is the power of vibrancy, creativity, joy, and inspiration. While the mechanisms of metaphysical principles here have been in place since the dawn of time, it is our purest intention to continue this work that began to gain prominence at the beginning of the 19th century in the New Thought Movement.

What are you Manifesting?

You may have noticed on the front cover this very powerful question. Ask yourself this to begin reading with some basic intentions and ideas of what you desire. Just as we would teach you, we are *acting as if* and actively demonstrating how to imprint the Universe with the vibration of success, thus the questions.

In the years before Jim Carrey became a superstar, he wrote himself a check for $10 million dollars and added "for acting services rendered". He carried it in his wallet from that day forth until the abundance and recognition that he desired started to manifest in his life. This act of setting an almighty intention contributed to his success eventually growing to fruition. As witnessed, the Universe responds to what is radiated energetically.

Your Journey Begins Now

Start it from a place of love and gratitude, knowing that as you read you will find resonance with what you are in alignment with in this point of time.

You will find yourself beginning to develop a story through direct experience of your intended reality. As you do, we will be here waiting with expectant joy and an open heart to see what you have to share with the world as well.

Until then, we will look forward to hearing all about your own adventures in manifesting.

With Love and Gratitude,
Älska

About Älska

Älska is the combined energies of Sarah Prout and Sean Patrick Simpson. The company name means *Love* and was received as gentle guidance one evening after a very intense session of laughter and joy.

You say it like this: 'elsh-ka' – which is slightly different than the original Scandinavian pronunciation of their verb (which means *to love*).

Sean and Sarah were prompted from within to start a metaphysical publishing company based on their mutual adoration of Universal truth and passion for writing. Hence, Älska was created!

http://www.alskapublishing.com

THE MANIFESTING COURSE

Get The Manifesting Course and join the Adventures in Manifesting community to connect with other like-minded and inspired individuals:

www.AdventuresInManifesting.org

Share Your Experience

Has a particular story, insight or teaching stood out to you?

We'd love to hear about your experience, so feel free to get in touch and let us know. You can e-mail us at:

feedback@adventuresinmanifesting.org

Additionally, with the intention and desire to share stories and teachings from all walks of life, we'd like to invite you to potentially be a part of one of the next *Adventures in Manifesting* titles.

Stories of all topics about manifesting are welcome (success, spirituality, health, happiness, wealth, love, prosperity, inner guidance, achieving dreams, overcoming obstacles, etc.)

If chosen as a top submission, we will get in touch directly to invite you to be a part of one of our next *Adventures in Manifesting* titles.

Please go to www.AdventuresInManifesting.org to share your experience (not to mention join the course and community, as well as find the hard copy, Kindle and iBook versions of other titles in the series).

Enjoy!

A TALE OF TRUE LOVE

Sean Patrick Simpson and Sarah Prout

"I'm going to put a message in a bottle, throw it in the ocean and see if it gets to the person I want to send it to one day." ~ @sarahprout via Twitter, October 1st 2009.

"Sarah, I'll be sure to go to the beach every day and look for a bottle then." ~ @vpsean (Sean Patrick Simpson) replied via Twitter on the same day.

Sarah: We met on Twitter in early 2009 from opposite ends of the planet. A little over a year later, Sean flew from Hollywood to meet me (in Australia) where we spent eleven blissful days remembering our deep soul connection and discovering that there was a Divine plan in the process of unfolding.

On the day we met, a vibrant rainbow arched over the road from the ocean as we drove home. We knew one another as if we had the spiritual recognition of spending lifetimes upon lifetimes together.

Our lives to this date had traveled a very parallel path of lessons with different backdrops and characters, nevertheless the same. We both loved metaphysics and spiritual teachings. We both believed that you create your own reality by using the power of manifesting, but not even in our wildest dreams could we have anticipated how our lives would unfold.

Twin Flames

We later discovered through a series of ethereal events that we are twin flames. Twin flames have been described in literature, philosophical texts, and spiritual doctrines as a single soul that's been split in two into the masculine and feminine counterparts. Each half is the other soul's counterpart, or *twin*, that is the exact polar opposite. When the twin souls unite it is for the completion of oneness. Their purpose together is one of service and we believe ours has to do with creating Älska Publishing and the Adventures in Manifesting series.

The twin flame theory is not a new idea at all. In fact, it has existed for thousands upon thousands of years. Plato mused about twin souls in the Symposium. His writings are philosophical about the nature of love and date back to 385-380 BCE.

Beyond the label you choose to put on two people who are clearly meant to be together though… *we are in love.*

It's a love that is unconditional, full of passion, joy, laughter, creativity, friendship, commitment, and divine pursuit of creating a life together. This is the love we want you to have and know you can experience.

Like you, we've had our own unique life experiences. We weren't granted with any extra special manifesting ability to find the one we could create true love with. We've also had our fair share of heartache as well.

Back to the Beginning

To give you a little background on our union, let's rewind to 2010.

We had been online friends for a little over a year. As mentioned, we met on Twitter and bonded over our love for the Law of Attraction and other metaphysical principles. Then one fine day we fell madly, deeply, and blissfully in love. We had a *knowing* and intrinsic recognition that we were supposed to be together. It was truly a surrendered process.

There was only one problem: we lived on opposite sides of the world. Sean was in California and I was in Noosa Heads, Australia.

During our first eleven days in person together, Sean wrote in our love journals a short story of our journey to finding each other. While the entirety of the love story hasn't been published yet, we'd like to share this letter from our most private journals with you.

As you read, we want you to imagine this story is about the union you will be having with the soul mate or twin flame you're attracting. Or alternatively, imagine it rekindling the love you already share with your life partner.

Sean: From the Love Journals

Once upon a time there was a man and a woman who were destined to be together. At the time of their meeting, they were perfect for each other. Everything about him was reflected in her, and everything about her was reflected in him.

…The way they laugh.

…The way they care.

…The way they love.

…The way they learn.

…The way they express.

…The way they cry.

Everything.

They were soul mates meant to find each other and begin a life of co-creation and manifestation, creating wonders through the intention of their souls and power of their thoughts.

Since the moment of their individual conception, they started the journey of attracting all the experiences they needed in their life to prepare them for their life together.

You see, they made an agreement. An agreement with the Universe which said:

> *"In this lifetime, we will be together once again. But first, we must learn some of the hardest lessons a person could go through. We must experience the natural pains of life that most all incur. But for our journey, in the midst of these experiences we must learn the lessons that are meant to be learned, for the Universe will continue to throw*

back to us the same challenges and experiences where learning & growing was meant to occur, over and over again as it does with every human being.

For us though, until those lessons are learned, we will not be together. The pains and tribulations that are faced with each of those experiences must be learned young in life so that we may co-create the life of love and beauty we are meant to create with one another. Until those lessons are learned, we will have things in place that will prevent us from being together and it will be up to us to find within all the powers we need to learn and evolve so we can find each other.

With each learned lesson, our magnetism towards one another will be charged, and when the time is right... when we have learned the lessons we were meant to and when we have learned what we have to, to co-create in the highest vibration possible, we will find each other.

And we will recognize each other, know we have finally found each other, and a new life will be born.

For we will no longer be just individuals on separate paths, for the combining of two soul mates creates an entity far more powerful than that of two individuals.

And that will be the driving force behind our love and life.

And with that force, we will begin to create magic.

A new set of mysteries, wonders and journeys will be embarked upon together..."

And so Sarah and Sean were born on opposite sides of the world and set in place... ready to take on the challenges of the world so that they could once again be together.

How would it occur? No one knew exactly how. Not even the essence of their souls did.

What their essence did know though was that they would do everything they could to find each other. They would take on all the challenges they had to.

They would go through all the pain and suffering they had to experience to become the individuals who were so resonant with each other that no possible force in the Universe – not the opinions of others or the miles through waters – could stop them from creating a life together.

In the year 2010, Sean Patrick Simpson and Sarah Prout found each other.

And this is their love story.

Back to The Present

I remember writing this within days of Sarah and I meeting in person. It came out in one steady stream, almost as though someone else was writing it. The energy we had been experiencing together was *out of this world.* And it was this energy I was tuned into while sitting there, having this flow through me.

It's a funny thing thinking back about when we first met online. We didn't think of our relationship as being anything more than friendship. How could we? We were on opposite sides of the world, Sarah was married (a marriage soon to end in disaster) and we were on our own career paths. Plus, we lived an entire ocean apart!

Over the year though we would find ourselves connecting more and more, confiding in each other some of our deepest experiences and closely kept secrets. Thousands of miles away, *we were becoming close.*

By around April to May 2010, it was as though the volume dial on our magnetism towards one another was suddenly being turned up. The idea of meeting in person became irresistible.

To that date though, we still had not spoken beyond the realms of Twitter or e-mail.

It's crazy, right? Two people falling in love before even meeting or speaking to one another verbally. Yet it happened. And spontaneously I chose to purchase a plane ticket to Australia with only about 10 days to spare before the trip.

Are you crazy? What if it doesn't work out? What about her kids? What if it 'does' work out, then what? You live in two different countries! What are you thinking?

They were valid questions I was bombarded with from people. But I don't play that game. The *what if* game. I go where I'm guided and, more than ever, I was feeling my inner guidance system telling me to go to Australia.

My friends weren't the only ones the *what if bug* got a hold of though. It was Sarah too.

Ten Days Before My Flight to Australia

Sarah:

Dear Sean,

Hello my lovely friend. We talked for 3 hours! Oh man. I wanted to keep talking.

Well here goes…

I feel a strong connection to you. I'm not sure what it is. And here's the thing.

You come to Australia. We have the BEST time like we know we're going to have. And then what? My heart gets broken because we live on opposite ends of the planet? Are we setting ourselves up for hurt?

I could see you today and I just wanted to be with you. I wanted to leap into that screen and touch you. That feeling is bad. We've talked only twice and I feel like I want to be cuddled by you. Held. And close. There's a familiarity there that I just adore. I'm not sure what it is, but it makes me miss you.

Anyway, just thought you should know my thoughts…

I had a long response to that e-mail. One of the main highlights though was:

Sean:

Love, there are so many 'what if's,' and when it comes down to it, we don't have the slightest clue of what's going to happen. It's kind of like life though, right? So the question then is, where do we turn to? Do we turn towards fear and let that determine our actions in everything we do from here on out, or do we let the higher vibration, that love and magnetism guide us through those unknowns?

We chose to align with the higher vibration.

Today, Sarah and I are actively co-creating the life of our dreams. Together we have learned so much from each other. And there is still so much more to learn. Today, our love story is still unfolding each and every day. Our photo has been placed on the front page of the Tiffany & Co. website to inspire people to find true love around the globe, and we have hundreds of manifesting students and authors that have joined our mission.

Where will the roads lead us from here? I'll let myself from two years ago share that with you…

Three Days Before my Flight to Australia

Subject: Sarah, Where Will the Roads Lead Us?

You know, I have no idea.

All I know is that I love you so much.

I feel like I've found my soul mate. And, the only reason I haven't admitted to having fallen yet is because of that slightest bit of caution, since we still have yet to meet.

But to be quite honest, I do believe I've fallen in love with you; madly, deeply, passionately. And I just want to be with you. I want to love you, hold you… and never let you go.

Who knows where the roads are about to lead us? Will there be challenges? Absolutely. Life wouldn't be the way it's meant to be without it.

I am confident though everything that's meant to happen will happen. And as long as we stay true to our highest selves, everything will fall in place.

I love you Sarah, and I want to find a way for us to be together… forever.

About the Authors

Sarah Prout and Sean Patrick Simpson are bestselling authors and new media publishers of the Adventures in Manifesting series. Their authentic and charismatic approach to teaching metaphysical studies has inspired students around the globe. With a strong social media fan base, the twin flame couple have shared their joyful journey with thousands.

Together they believe in the power of connection to engage an audience from the screen to the stage. Their mission is to teach others how to create a life filled with love and how to manifest their dreams.

You can connect with Sarah and Sean personally, as well as the other authors and readers of this book through the Adventures in Manifesting community.

http://www.adventuresinmanifesting.org

http://www.seanpatricksimpson.com

http://www.sarahprout.com

HEALING THROUGH SELF-TALK

Evelyn Lim

For a long time, I was engaged in an incessant stream of negative self-talk. Similar to a broken record, my self-talk would play non-stop. But because I wasn't tuned in, it had not occurred to me how debilitating and destructive this could be. Only when I started to keep a journal of my very thoughts, did I realize how much I had been putting myself down.

Eventually, I realized that the underlying problem was an issue of *self-love*.

I did have positive thoughts. They were, however, mostly overshadowed and smothered by the negative ones. The stream of self-talk had looked something like this: *I am such a failure. I suck. I am okay. I look too fat. I am too thin. I am so slow. I am an idiot. No, I'm not an idiot. I'm too short. I am ugly. I hate my nose. It is okay to be ordinary. I never do things right. I was born this way. I am hopeless. I am not worthy.*

I am not lovable.

During more intense periods, my self-criticisms would be harsh, crippling, and harmful at best. Even when I made a mistake, I would find it particularly challenging to practice self-forgiveness. I was pretty much stuck in the past as I refused to let go of blame. Oddly enough, I craved approval from others but was unable to give myself the same level of acceptance.

When I started reviewing what I had recorded in my journal, I discovered how depleted, dispirited, and sore I was. It dawned on me as to why I had never felt fully well. With the negative background noise inside my head, it was hard to function successfully on the outside. I also found out that, during the nights, my self-talk would usually get worse. Much worse. The emotional upheaval on the inside contributed to external struggles with insomnia and eczema. I could not sleep well due to physical itching and stress; symptomatic of the irritation that I felt inside.

As soon as I made a serious commitment to the self, my journey became one of rebuilding my inner world. Maintaining a personal journal was an effective form of therapy, which helped me gain greater self-awareness. I made the attempt to slow down deliberately, so that I could *catch* my own thoughts. From analyzing the pages of my journal, it gradually became obvious to me that I had been experiencing the core issue of insufficient self-love. Instead of care and compassion, I had been directing anger, blame, and frustration inwards.

I was simply not happy with who I was.

What is it Like for You?

If you are like the vast majority of people, chances are you have been saying nasty things to yourself. You are likely to greet yourself with harsh judgments about your looks, abilities, performance, and, in fact, everything. You may have the habit of focussing on the parts that are wrong, imperfect, or not good enough about yourself. For the record, studies show that for the average person, 80% of self-evaluations reflect negative thoughts about oneself with the remaining 20% being positive.

You are engaged in negative self-talk because there is some part about yourself that you are not happy with. While your unhappiness could offer a motivational impetus for you to pursue growth, excessive negative self-talk can obstruct your path to overall wellness and success. On the extreme side of things, you may even shred yourself to pieces with your criticisms because you are unable to accept your imperfections.

After I started sharing my ideas of self-love on my blog, more than a thousand readers across the world responded by emailing me their own stories. This went on for the best part of three years. I realized that I was not the only one who had faced problems with loving myself. In fact, as my findings subsequently reveal, self-love issues do not differentiate between people: they cut across and invaded all cultures, countries, religions, and ages. There are people all over the world who experience internal conflicts, which get mirrored in external events, everyday.

Consequences of Low Self Love

Whether you love yourself unconditionally or not, there can be many consequences. Both experiences affect you at all levels of mind, body and spirit.

You possibly feel fundamentally flawed. Your belief is that *I am not good enough to be lovable*. By constantly belittling yourself, you suffer from an inferiority complex. Thus, you find it difficult to develop healthy relationships, attract wealth, or become successful.

Physical symptoms start to show up when you are not emotionally stable. Furthermore, there is an increased chance of developing problems at the level of the heart. You may also take on destructive eating patterns or addictive behavior in an effort to avoid the pain of self-rejection. Subjecting the body to physical abuse is a very common consequence.

Internally, you experience a sense of separation from your true self. It happens when you starve yourself from that spiritual need we call love. Thus, you feel disconnected, lost, and confused. You become unable to align yourself with the higher purpose of your existence. It becomes ever so hard for you to feel alive when you are in such a state; you feel that you *exist*, but are not *alive*.

With little love, life loses its meaning.

Consequences of Healthy Self Love

On the other hand, if you have a healthy sense of self-love, you accept and embrace yourself completely. You are able to see the best in yourself. You have the confidence to pursue your dreams and goals because you know that you are *good enough*. By feeling secure, you have the core belief that you have a place in this world. You also forgive yourself whenever you make a mistake, and are able to pick yourself up quickly whenever you encounter a setback.

By loving yourself, you choose to undertake healthy behaviors, wise decisions, and inspired actions. You practice excellent self-care for your body. You make sensible food choices, exercise regularly, and take breaks every now and then.

Loving yourself leads to integrating yourself into spiritual wholeness. You realize that even whilst you may be humanly imperfect, you are complete at the soul level. Through integration, you discover that, essentially, you are Divine love. You are your basic nature.

You are one and the same as Source.

Obviously, self-love rests on a continuum. The vast majority of us are at neither ends of the extreme. On my part, I was not engaged in self-destructive behaviors like drinking or taking drugs but I certainly subjected myself to a fair amount of criticism. The inability to love myself sufficiently affected my level of wellness. My subsequent discovery has shown me plainly that I can experience greater happiness, joy, and abundance simply by loving myself more.

Release Fear in Your Mind

Your inner talk is most likely negative if you have little self-love. Self-talk that is based on fear creates negative energetic disruptions. An inner war inside you is waged because you are compelled to live with yourself, even though you detest seeing your own image in the mirror. You find it hard to experience peace because you are in vibrational disharmony on the inside.

The thing is, you play out a life script based on your internal self-talk. What you say and believe internally is what drives your actions, habits, and behavior. It is possible to become so trapped in the incessant stream of your own internal talk that it becomes the only reality you know. And so you identify yourself with all the negative labels such as *failure, freak, bad ass, loser, wimp,* or *dumb* that you have used on yourself. An over-identification causes you to lose touch with who you really are.

Fear, as much as love, is energy. However, psychological fear is not real. It is an illusion. Fear holds you back from loving yourself. Your capacity to give fully to yourself is reduced when you are in fear. Fear creates the belief that you are separated from your inner being. Your internal conflict causes you to project fear on the outside. Consequently, you find yourself manifesting more fear-based circumstances.

As it is often said, *your mind creates your reality.*

Hence, if you want things to change externally for the better, bring *awareness* to your internal dialogue. Awareness casts light to the shadows that fear lurks around. You face up to what has been holding you back internally. However, as you go through this inward process, avoid adding another round of criticism. The last thing you want is to attack yourself even more. Should you attack yourself with more judgment, it would tantamount to adding salt to an already open wound.

In the meantime, stay present to yourself without the need to censure, judge, or criticize. You practice non-attachment even as you review your past. You are likely to begin experiencing energy shifts within a pure loving atmosphere. Free from mental torture, you enjoy a lightness of being.

Reawaken to Love in Your Heart

Things have started to change for me ever since I began practicing greater self-love. With increased awareness, I am more alert to my self-talk. Instead of using disempowering words, I choose to be more supportive inwardly. I am more willing to treat myself with greater compassion. Gradually, I find myself enjoying my own company. I am this happy because I have become best friends with myself.

If you have been trapped in a negative state for a long time, then you will need to learn how to love yourself unconditionally. In other words, self-love is to be a practice. It involves a holistic mind-body-spirit approach. You undertake actions to love yourself at every level. You are in full acceptance of yourself, regardless of any conditions. You also choose love over fear in every life situation. It may seem awkward at first to tell yourself *I love you* in the mirror, but as you seek alignment from within, making such an affirmation should start to feel natural.

Essentially, you hope to release the fear in your mind and to reawaken the love in your heart. Previously, you may not have been able to realize that inside of you, a deep loving reservoir exists. Fear clouds your mind from knowing deeply who you are. However, once you lift the veil of fear, layer upon layer, clarity emerges, and you reconnect spiritually from within. Your soul has incarnated to experience love in its many manifestations.

The Healing Power of Love

Love is a healing power that dissipates fear. Love makes your journey on Earth meaningful. There are many opportunities for you to love a little more each day. You can only know deeply what love is experientially. Love is joy in springtime, peace in a prayer, forgiveness in a smile, kindness in an act, intimacy in your relationship, and so on. Living from your heart is a powerful spiritual and physical experience that you can have. And it starts by loving yourself.

Love is your soul magnet. It is the vibration that enables you to magnetize the goodness in life. When you love yourself, you gain a radiant glow that shines from deep within. You become a luminary. Others cannot help but become drawn. Transformed, they feel inspired to love themselves too. They go on to becoming shining luminaries themselves. You find yourself sharing a deep connection with others because love unites. Thus, just by loving yourself, you have brought about more love in the world.

Ultimately, through love, life responds with an abundance of miracles.

About the Author

Evelyn Lim is passionate about helping others lead a fulfilling life. She intends to do this by first creating greater holistic self-love awareness. A life coach, she is the author of *Self-Love Secrets: How to Love Yourself Unconditionally*. She wrote the book after receiving a thousand emails from readers who faced tremendous difficulties with loving themselves. Her book reveals the inner obstacles that keep abundance at bay for the vast majority of people in the world.

Evelyn Lim is also the author of another book, *Abundance Alchemy: Journey of Gold* and the program, *Life Vision Mastery*. Professionally, she is certified as a master neuro-linguistic practitioner, emotional freedom technique practitioner, an intuitive consultant, and a vision board counselor.

She currently resides in Singapore with her family, including two lovely girls.

http://www.abundancetapestry.com

LOVE AT FIRST SIGHT

Jonathan Yudis

Her name was Victoria, but I did not know that at the time. Nor did I know time itself when I first stood in her presence. I should apologize in advance for the hopeless romanticism of this story, but I swear to you that it's all true.

This is a story about love; true love.

I was a twenty-two year old male college-student at the height of my testosterone-fueled sexual prowess. Even though I was *playing the field* and dating multiple women at the time, one in particular named Karen, was very attracted to and interested in me. We had been on a few dates and while I was resistant to it becoming anything other than casual, she kept asking why we couldn't become a more serious couple.

I didn't want to say it at the time, but the truth was that while I liked her and we had fun together, I knew she simply wasn't *the one*.

Earlier that same year, my life began to change as I realized that there was something fundamentally empty about the entire dating process. Though I might have been young in age, I felt a deep yearning to find what I had long dreamed of in terms of a *true love* and *life partner*. All I knew was that I understood in my gut how challenging life was and that I deeply desired to meet that one person whom I could journey through this life with in loving partnership.

For six months or so, before I went to bed every night, I'd been secretly praying to meet this person. That's right. Every single night.

"Dear God, thank you so much for all the blessings and Divine grace you bestow upon me daily. I know you know what's in my heart. Please believe my sincerity as I pray to meet *the one*. I know that she's out there! And I know you can help me find her. This life is such a mystery and can be such a struggle; I don't want to go through it alone."

Of course we are never really *alone*. But at the time, I was expressing this powerful desire to meet the woman of my dreams: The one that would inspire, understand and accept me, and go on this incredible journey of life together always rooted in love.

As far as meetings go, ours was about as random as they come!

After an evening of bar hopping, Karen and I were strolling along Avenue B in lower Manhattan at 3 a.m. when, suddenly, this woman came running out of a local bar. She and Karen looked at each other and stopped because they recognized one another. I didn't know it at the time but, as it turned out, they were only vague acquaintances with each other from New York University's film department.

It soon became apparent that their familiarity was slightly awkward. I specifically remember Karen asking her: "What's it like being Ralph Bakshi's daughter?"

I had never heard of him, but I later found out that Victoria's father is a legend in the world of animation, a brilliant filmmaker, and a fine artist. At this point in the story, I must point out that these details are what I would classify as the 3D reality of our first meeting.

I believe that life is multi-dimensional and holographic in nature, meaning that there are an infinite number of dimensions of existence or reality occurring simultaneously. Depending on various states of mind, such as our focus, awareness, and frequency of our consciousness, we can perceive or experience the different dimensions being played out or projected upon the holographic or cosmic motion picture screen.

If we are fortunate, occasionally we have what are often referred to as *peak experiences* or moments of profound awareness, understanding, and realization. These experiences deeply affect and sometimes fundamentally alter the course of our lives.

Being in the presence of Victoria and first laying my eyes on her was definitely one of these peak experiences in my life.

Like all moments, which penetrate into truth, they are difficult to put into words. I know that parts of me, like my physical flesh and body were standing there with Karen and Victoria on the street of Avenue B, and part of me was aware of this the entire time. But there was also another part of me, perhaps my soul, or my light or etheric body, which leaped instantaneously in this moment. It was like a blast of combustion, an explosion of light and emotion, much like two stars colliding in space!

There are times when we are filled with so much emotion that it feels as if we cannot contain it; as if we are really not sure what is going to happen. This was one of those moments. I felt as, if in an instant, I traveled through the vast galaxies of our cosmos and into the pure bright light of the sun! I saw a lifetime of specific images of my life flash before my eyes, not in any particular order or even limited to the past, present, or future. The amazing thing was that somehow I wasn't just seeing these images, but I was experiencing them as well, and Victoria was present in so many of them with me. In this instant, I knew with every ounce of my being that she was *the One*. She was the answer to my prayer and the woman of my dreams, standing right in front of me in the flesh.

And what flesh it was: soft and delicate; the epitome of everything that I defined as beauty down to a T! How amazing, and what a tremendous gift, to see this woman I had yearned to meet standing before me in the exact physical expression of my dreams. Profound gratitude and awe are poor substitutes to describe what was going through me in that moment.

And she was blue! Not her skin, but her aura or the energy field around her was an incredible electric blue, much like the glow of the earth's atmosphere when you see it in photographs taken from space.

With all this going on in that instant, it's understandable that I was unable to say anything. I simply stood there completely speechless.

Victoria was clearly a bit confused and flabbergasted by Karen's question about how it felt to be this famous film director's daughter; a question which had probably been thrown at her countless times as a student in the film program at NYU. Though I was silent, I shrugged, as if to say: "Sorry Karen just asked you an awkward question which makes you feel uncomfortable." And I smiled as if to say: "Hi, here I am. You might not recognize me, but I recognize *you*. Thank you for being alive... I love you!"

While I went beyond my ordinary perception of time and space in that one moment, as sure as it arrived, it was gone, and I found myself walking along the street again with Karen. She knew me well enough to know that something had changed.

She stopped and said, "What's going on with you? You're acting weird." And in no way was my reply intended to be mean. On the contrary, I felt a sense of liberation in finally being able to be completely truthful with her. I said, "That girl, that girl we just bumped into, that's going to be my girlfriend."

Dumbfounded and upset, Karen replied: "What? Victoria Bakshi? You don't even know her."

I didn't say anything else. I just shrugged and smiled.

To myself, I thought: "Victoria Bakshi. Thank you. Thank you for telling me the name of the woman of my dreams. And yes, I do know her. I might not know her stories or what music she likes, but I know her in all the ways that matter to the heart and soul. And in these matters, I now know that we have lived a lifetime together."

Suffice it to say that this was my last official date with Karen, but just the beginning of my life with Victoria.

Flash forward twenty years to the writing of this story, Victoria not only became my girlfriend but, a few years later, also my wife. Many of those specific images I had witnessed and experienced in that timeless instant have now become memories that we have shared together. Perhaps the greatest blessing of our union is not those images manifested, but the incredibly wonderful children and family we have created together. Fortunately there are still a few images that have not yet come to fruition, which gives me even more to look forward to!

Just in case this love at first sight story might sound too much like a fantasy, I should mention that there is a definite distinction between the timeless realms of love and light, and the 3D realm of ordinary perception and physical reality.

Though I had experienced this monumental moment of our soul connection and life together at that first encounter, Victoria's experience might have been simply seeing a funny looking bald guy who just shrugged and smiled.

After that night, even with more prayers being answered and magically seeing or bumping into Victoria many times over the next several weeks, it took months to develop a friendship and nearly one year of old-fashioned courtship before our first kiss atop the Empire State Building's observation deck. After all that time, I was nearly desperate to consummate our relationship and I knew that if we shared a romantic kiss, it would prove that we were much more than just friends.

So I turned to her and said, "Did you know that when two people kiss at this height there is an electric shock?"

She replied, "Please don't tell me you just said that."

Some people might take that as a rejection, but thanks to that timeless moment so many months prior, I refused to take no for an answer and kissed her anyway! Eureka! I think there was an electric shock. Otherwise, how could we have made it so joyously through all of the ups and downs and life-changes and still be together?!

Like any other relationship and partnership, we do have our problems and issues, so experiencing love at first sight doesn't mean our life together has been without its challenges, though, in our hearts, we are infinitely connected. We love each other to the extent that we can accept and appreciate our differences, and regardless of how we grow and change, we continually endeavor to bring out the best in each other.

Love might be a four letter word, but it's an infinite force and the ultimate expression in our Universe. It's easy to become cynical and lose touch with this grounding essence which is the alpha and the omega; the beginning and the end. With this in mind, I wanted to share this story with the intention that the same waves and currents of love which have graced my life will flow through my heart and reach you through these very words.

So in the name of this eternal mystery we call *true love*, I leave you with this new prayer, one which is already being fulfilled as I write and you read these words: "Dear God, May each of us find, know, and live the true love that surpasses all understanding."

About the Author

Jonathan Yudis is an evolutionary and award-winning filmmaker, author, artist, actor, speaker, and yogi.

He leads inspirational seminars and has taught yoga & spirituality in the U.S. since 1995. His books include *The Thought That Changed My Life Forever* and is a co-author of *Adventures in Manifesting: Success & Spirituality*.

Jonathan is president and creative director at Infinite Entertainment Now, a visionary media company currently producing the holiday comedy *Aloha Santa*. He holds a BFA from New York University and an MFA from the American Film Institute. His film, television, and web work has garnered multiple Telly Awards and the student Academy Award.

As a graduate of the Shift Networks *Agents of Conscious Evolution*, Jonathan is collaborating on a series of simultaneous international meditations on 12/22/12 and beyond to foster global unity and harmony.

Jonathan lives with an ongoing attitude of gratitude on the island of Maui with his wife and children.

http://www.jonathanyudis.com (1)

http://www.onebillionoms.com (2)

THE ROMANTIC MYSTERIES

Marianne Williamson

The common wisdom goes like this: That the myth of *some enchanted evening*, when all is awash with the thrill of connection and the aliveness of new romance, is actually a delusion; a hormonally manufactured lie. That soon enough, reality will set in and lovers will awaken from their mutual projections, discover the psychological work involved in two people trying to reach across the chasm of real life separateness, and come to terms at last with the mundane sorrows of human existence and intimate love.

In this case, the common wisdom is a lie.

From a spiritual perspective, the scenario above is upside down. From a spiritual perspective, the original high of a romantic connection is thrilling because it is true. It is in fact the opposite of delusion. For in a quick moment, a gift from the gods, we are likely to suspend our judgment of the other, not because we are temporarily insane but because we are temporarily sane. We are having what you might call a mini-enlightenment experience. Enlightenment is not unreal; enlightenment – or pure love – is all that is real. Enlightenment is when we see not as through a glass darkly, but truly face to face.

What is unreal is what comes after the initial high, when the personality self reasserts itself and the wounds and triggers of our human ego form a veil across the face of love. The initial romantic high is not something to outgrow, so much as something to earn admittance back into, this time not as an unearned gift of Cupid's arrows, but as a consequence of the real work of the psychological and spiritual journey. The romantic relationship is a spiritual assignment, presenting an opportunity for lovers and would-be lovers to burn through our own issues and forgive the other theirs, so together we can gain re-entrance to the joyful realms of our initial contact that turn out to have been real love after all.

Our problem is that most of us rarely have a psychic container strong enough to stand the amount of light that pours into us when we have truly seen, if even for a moment, the deep beauty of another. The problem we have is not that in our romantic fervor we fall into a delusion of oneness; the problem is that we then fall into the delusion of separateness. And those are the romantic mysteries; the almost blinding light when we truly see each other, the desperate darkness of the ego's blindness, and the sacred work of choosing the light of mutual innocence when the darkness of anger, guilt, and fear descend.

About the Author

Marianne Williamson is an internationally acclaimed spiritual author and lecturer. Six of her ten published books have been *New York Times* Bestsellers. Four of these have been #1 *New York Times* Bestsellers. *A Return to Love* is considered a must-read of The New Spirituality. A paragraph from that book, beginning with, *"Our deepest fear is not that we are inadequate. Our deepest fear is that we are powerful beyond measure..."* – often misattributed to Nelson Mandela's Inaugural address – is considered an anthem for a contemporary generation of seekers.

Marianne's books include *The Age of Miracles, Everyday Grace, A Woman's Worth, Illuminata, Healing the Soul of America*, and *The Gift of Change*.

Marianne's latest *New York Times* Bestseller is *A Course in Weight Loss: 21 Spiritual Lessons for Surrendering Your Weight Forever*. *A Course in Weight Loss* was selected by Oprah to be one of her favorite things in 2010.

http://www.marianne.com

7 LOVE DYNAMICS START WITH LOVE OF SELF

Sherrie Rose

As The Love Linguist®, most people come to me seeking answers for intimate love relationships. Of the 7 love dynamics, five of those are intimate and two are personal ones, the latter being love of self and love of God.

Love of self is for some people the same as love of God. Since some people are atheists, these two love dynamics are separated simply for the purpose of sharing information that would appeal to a person on the path of self-growth and discovery, regardless of whether they have a spiritual inkling or chosen faith to express love of the Divine.

The 7 love dynamics start with love of self, so let's look at the linguistics behind the first word: dynamic.

Dynamic relates to energy or objects in motion often marked by intensity and vigor. The intensity is varied, which is what makes it, by definition, dynamic. Dynamics are characterized by continuous change, activity, or progress. Progress is what is needed for transformation; transformation to become a better version of yourself.

That's part of self-love.

Next, the word *self*.

Self is the total, essential, or particular being of a person; the individual separate from any other. It is the essential qualities distinguishing one person from another and one's consciousness of one's own being or identity; the ego.

Now about *ego*.

Self-love does not mean the *egotist* expression of self-love or conceit that goes along with the idea of *I am better than you*, but quite the opposite. It is a healthy honorable self-respect and acknowledgement with a clear understanding that what I see in myself I can also recognize in another.

Love of self may involve ego, but *true* love of self is not egotistical or self-absorbed. Self-love is not arrogance, narcissism, or self-glory. We all long for love, and self-love is attractive because it shows up in confidence, a feeling of worthiness, and most often in humility and modesty.

Love of self is a dynamic expression.

The emotional attributes of love of self are expressed in these ways: kindness, benevolence, discipline, awe, beauty, harmony, compassion, endurance, ambition, humility, and self-leadership. Self-love is a dynamic force of success in your life that keeps you true to your highest ideals.

You maintain your self-esteem when you are humble. You acknowledge your talents and strengths and apply them for a higher purpose and not only to satisfy your own needs. Humility in love of self is the key to transcendence; to reach beyond you.

When I love myself I can be grateful for my own life and acknowledge what a sacred gift life truly is. When I respect myself, I honor who I am. When you love yourself you feel no need to harm or hurt any other living being because you want to protect and cherish.

Your self-identity and your purpose are the keys to your self-love.

Recently, I shared time with a friend, Lauren. She had just lost the love of her life after a four-year battle with cancer. Apart from the grief, she told me she felt lost. She had no idea of who she was. She felt out of sorts. She said she was no longer in a relationship, no longer a caretaker, no longer any of the *roles* she had previously been labeled.

We went through an exercise where she could re-invent herself. By removing the guilt-causing thoughts from her early childhood and adult experiences, she could start clean so to speak. Then by clarifying the things that she was passionate about, outlining her strong points and weak points, soon she felt her sense of inner security come back and new self-identity born. She began to forgive and trust herself again.

Self-worth is a tenuous feeling. If a failure comes your way, your self-worth and love of self may falter. There will always be another assault on your self-esteem because that is just a part of living.

Get up and dust yourself off. Remember your emotional health depends on a warm, wonderful feeling you have about yourself. Strive to be your best self and devote yourself to your personal self-improvement. Self-confidence gives you the faith in your own possibilities and creative pursuits.

You travel on the road to emotional, mental, and spiritual health when you seek to know and appreciate yourself. When you know and love yourself, you *truly* come alive!

Love thyself: Leviticus 19:18. The full biblical sentence reads: "Thou shalt not avenge, nor bear any grudge against the children of thy people, but thou shalt love thy neighbor as thyself."

The absence or the poor understanding of the importance of self-love affects everything. How we relate and respect others show up in our words and actions. If you continuously and negatively judge yourself by the results you have, or have not, achieved in the past, rather than the lessons you have learned and the growth you have experienced in the present, you short-change yourself and others who interact with you.

When we truly embrace our ancestral wisdom *love thyself*, we won't need to chase relationships trying to find self-love through love for another person. Self-love can help eliminate the expectation, frustration, and disappointment about our mistaken notion of this human emotion of love.

Start with yourself and your love of self. Then, you will embrace all of your human relationships from a stand point of sharing the abundance of what you already have, rather than the need to get something you believe to lack.

Self-initiative is a form of self-love because you are taking action. A slight twist on a familiar phrase:

"God helps those who love themselves."

Benjamin Franklin, one of the Founding Fathers of the United States, in 1736 used the original phrase with the words, "help themselves" in his almanac. Franklin believed in God and also believed that

God did not intervene in the earth's affairs, so all responsibility was incumbent upon individual people.

We must be self-sufficient. You cannot expect that another person is going to take care of you or love you. If intimate love comes into your life it may be enhanced if you have well-established self-love. Many times in a love relationship you can grow together as well as develop individually. There is much overlap in love. We don't live life with experiences happening in neat order with perfect timing. Family love, self-love, intimate love, and personal and business friendships are all intertwined.

Self-love is Universal. Self-love is the ultimate will of mankind. Various self-motivators in life such as pleasure, power, meaning, purpose, and creativity are all aspects of self-love. Self-love helps the need to fulfill an inner drive towards personal dignity and self-worth.

A deep sense of self worth gives rise to self confidence. Self confidence is a personal belief you have which gives you the ability to triumph over difficulties and which leads you to success. You may get assurance from others but you do not need external assurance from other people when you are filled with self-love.

Tap into your own personal power with love of self. A solid relationship with yourself has benefits in all areas of your life. Your feelings and attitude about yourself keep you going when you hit a rough patch and keep you even keeled when you are soaring high. These feelings may also bring you down if you have a tendency towards self-sabotage which is in opposition of self-love.

"The longest relationship you have is with yourself."

I came up with The Love Bucket® concept in terms of intimate love and desire, both of which are intangible feelings and emotions. That's why The Love Bucket is a concept and not a physical bucket. True love of self is when you have a sense of inner-peace and you feel *full* without the desperate need for someone else to fill you in. You know you are *whole* and do not need a better half or someone else to complete you.

Fill your own Love Bucket first.

At certain times of the year, the images of romance are prevalent such as Valentine's Day. Holidays often create pangs of longing to be in a love relationship. If you are single, that's the perfect time to treat and honor yourself with the love you deserve.

There are many things you can do to lift your spirits and show yourself some self-love and fill your heart, mind, and activities.

Here are a few ideas for self-love which will take alone or in combination of thought, time, effort or money.

- Look at your wardrobe and put together a new outfit. Or buy some new clothes or get a haircut.

- Give yourself compliments. That's great self-talk. Give others compliments too. Be a good receiver when accepting compliments.

- Allow yourself to get embarrassed when you fail. Give yourself this permission as a form of self-love.

- Find a trustworthy friend or mentor or professional and share feelings that have been bottled up inside.

- Allow yourself to be *flawsome* (flawed plus awesome). Take risks and eliminate perfectionism.

- Get your health together and stand up proud and tall.

- Take on a creative project.

- Pick a challenge or create goals and achieve them, one step at a time.

- Join a community club (in real life, not just social media) and meet a person who you think is important to you in some way.

- Forgive yourself.

- Accept yourself.

- Believe in your success.

- Say *yes!* to yourself.

Other people, members of the opposite sex, and even animals are drawn to a person who loves him or herself. It is a *very* attractive quality.

When we love ourselves, we want to participate with others and share ourselves. What you manifest is a reflection of your inner thoughts and beliefs and your self-love. It takes great courage to love and you deserve to love yourself. So give yourself the gift of self-love.

For all the love you will ever need is already within yourself.

About the Author

Sherrie's Motto: The Real Currency is Relationship Riches.

Sherrie Rose, Liking Authority™ and Love Linguist® – is the founder of the Love Success Network. Sherrie's a master at networking and opening hearts and minds to connect people for love riches and epic business success.

International spokesperson for Love and Liking, she is a recognized expert, fast-paced visionary, Liking Authority™, fondly known as Lady Love Bucket, author, part-time technogeek, neuroamateur, speaker, interview host, spiritual entrepreneur, and full-time lover of life!

Sherrie has created programs on love and relationships and is fondly known for her trademark, filling The Love Bucket® and Relationship Riches™. Sherrie coined several terms and her favorite is *lovematism*.

Love starts with *liking* in all relationships, both business and personal. See what Sherrie is giving a "Likes Up" to in social media (hashtag #LikesUP).

http://www.asksherrierose.com

LIVE IN LOVE

Jeff Thibodeau

How would you live your life today if you knew it was your last? You would probably pay more attention to those everyday, but often overlooked, miracles like children laughing, wind whistling, and the moon rising. You would completely show up for every moment, cherishing every detail, and capturing every second. You would give more of yourself to the world and gratefully embrace more of what is given to you. You would live your life on purpose and be your best you. And most importantly, you would live your life with, and *in*, love.

But how do we do it? Love is something we all want to give and receive in our lives and we strive to manifest it every day. But it can be strangely elusive to find, in spite of our seeking.

Are You a Seeker or a Finder?

> *"Your task is not to seek for love,*
> *but merely to seek and find all the barriers within yourself*
> *that you have built against it."*
> ~Rumi~

How long have you been seeking love in your life without finding it? You keep searching, yearning, reaching, waiting, working, and grasping, but to no avail. I know; I've been there many times before. We all have. We want love from our families, our spouses, our kids, our friends, and sometimes from people we barely know. But even when we *do* get it, it doesn't quite fulfill us. So we keep looking or asking for more, and complaining when we can't find the abundance of love that we seek.

Have you ever thought about the irony and powerlessness in that? That as perpetual *seekers* we prevent ourselves from becoming the *finders* of the love we are looking for? Sometimes, when we focus single-mindedly on the goal and destination of our journey, we can unintentionally overlook the path we are walking on, which is made of a multitude of moments strung together, like notes composing a song. The song is the beautiful end result, but the individual notes are the true seeds of its creation; the life of its melody.

Perhaps you, like so many seekers, have been looking in the wrong direction. Instead of looking somewhere out on the horizon to the future or to other people, things, and circumstances in an effort to fulfill your desires, what would happen if you simply looked inside yourself? Can you imagine a reality in which you find all the love you need within you, and in every moment feel completely fulfilled even when your life circumstances are difficult?

It *is* possible.

I am not speaking in fluffy, esoteric terms. This is not rhetorical or hypothetical. It is real. You and everything you experience in life is composed of the essential energy of life: *true love*. Most people spend their lives searching for it outside themselves, missing its strong and silent presence within. The key to realizing it, to *finding* it, is to give your complete attention to each moment and everything that presents itself to you in life. When you do, true love blooms and makes itself known.

> *"Everything in the Universe is within you.*
> *Ask all from yourself."*
> ~Rumi~

When we pay mindful attention to the present moment, we reach *at-one-ment* with life and live in love. Individual consciousness moves beyond the limits of the separate self into the vastness that surrounds us, allowing the emergence of a boundless inner essence: love. So how do we learn to do that? I'm not talking about doing it some day in the future; I'm talking about doing it every day, starting now.

Meditation: The Path to Love

*"Meditate. Live purely. Be quiet. Do your work with mastery.
Like the moon, come out from behind the clouds! Shine."* ~Buddha~

The practice of paying complete attention to life in the present moment is called meditation. Meditation can be done anywhere anytime. It requires no particular belief, no guru, no special place, and no one but yourself. It is not an esoteric practice of monks on mountaintops. Rather, it is the simplest way to experience the love and life that defines you. Meditation practice includes three simple elements: posture, focus, and breathing.

Posture

The posture assumed during meditation can be either still or in motion. Still meditation is usually done while seated but can also be done standing or lying down. Moving meditation practices, such as martial arts and yoga, involve movement through a diverse sequence of postures. Good posture is important because it facilitates mental and physical stability, centeredness, strength, discipline, balance, focus, and proper breathing. The three most important physical aspects of good posture are centered balance, spinal alignment, and a strong but relaxed body. To assume a simple posture that you can achieve with ease, sit with your feet on the ground, spine erect, shoulders relaxed, arms resting on your thighs with palms up or down, and look straight ahead.

Focus

To focus is to place consistent and pinpointed attention of the body, mind, and spirit upon something while letting go of all distractions. During meditation practice, the object of focus is most often your breathing, but could also be a flame, word, mantra, idea, virtue, person, or deity. By focusing on one thing and constantly returning your wandering mind to it, you learn how to remain available to each moment that presents itself in life.

The breath is the simplest, most familiar, and most accessible object of focus. From our first cry at birth to our last gasp at death, it is with us and enlivens us every moment. Focusing on the breath brings our minds into rhythm with our bodies and with the present moment.

Breathing

There are many different meditation breathing techniques that you can try. However, it is best to keep it simple. Breathe through the nose in a normal, regular rhythm, keeping the lips closed, jaw relaxed, and teeth apart. Draw the breath in deeply but gently into the lower abdomen. Do not force it to expand; simply allow it to do so. Let your abdominal relaxation draw the breath down as if you were filling a water balloon from a faucet with very low water pressure. To help facilitate clearer focus, pay attention to the feel of the breath as it tickles the tip of your nose.

If you want, you can also try four-step breathing. Breathe in for a count of four, hold for a count of four, breath out for a count of four, hold for a count of four, and repeat. Keep the breathing easy and if you lose your focus on it, simply return to it and continue. Release all frustration and self-judgment. When your mind wanders, bring your attention back to your breath, over and over again with gentleness and a sense of surrender.

As you quiet your body and mind, you will notice a barrage of thoughts and feelings wash through you, pulling your attention towards them and away from your focus. Persistent meditation practice, however, builds a greater ability to remain focused in the midst of distractions. With consistent practice you will be able to detach your consciousness from these passing thoughts and feelings. It's kind of like stepping outside yourself, standing above and behind your mind, and watching how your personality operates from a higher vantage point.

Instead of getting caught up identifying yourself with your distractions, lost in the drama they create, you can learn to simply *observe* them. This ability to remain present and conscious, yet detached, will enable you to be loving and present even in your most troubling and uncomfortable situations.

Living and Loving Completely

*"I give myself completely to love," I said aloud and then slowly
started to walk across the burning embers, focused completely on each
step with the energy of my intention behind it.*

*When I got to the end, I felt great. But contrary to what
I had expected, my feet were slightly burned.*

I had not felt the pain until then.

*The epiphany for me was not simply that a focused spirit
and mind can transcend physical reality
but also that when you give yourself completely to love,
there are times when you will get burned by its intensity.*

It is part of living and loving completely.

Living in love is wonderful but it does not always mean you will float blissfully above life's challenges and pain. Rather, it means that you will give yourself completely to whatever presents itself, whether easy or difficult, and in doing so show up with your entire *self* for every precious moment of your life. When you do this, you go with the flow, neither chasing nor grasping life. You remain present for the process but detached from outcomes.

You live in love.

It is important to understand that being detached from a situation does not mean you are careless. Rather, it means you do not attach yourself too tightly to outcomes. It means you trust completely in the Universe and the perfect imperfection of life more than your own thoughts, feelings, and circumstances no matter how compelling they may be.

Meditation can help you place more attention on the present moment in spite of your comfort level. Bringing greater attention to any situation allows the opportunity for love to bring its healing, expansive energy to help calm the surface turbulence of changing circumstance and life challenges.

Ride the Tide

Whatever posture, focus, or breathing method we choose, when in a meditative state, things seem to happen by themselves in perfect order. There is abundant life energy moving through us but very little effort. We are perfectly calm, but alert and aware. Everything flows easily to its natural result, just as a river runs to the sea, and we go with the flow. We become vehicles through which the energy of life – pure love – expresses itself.

> *At age twenty-eight I was working in the city and*
> *yearning for my home on the Cape.*
> *The concrete was stale and so was my spirit.*
> *I went home one weekend and saw a late movie that*
> *moved me to tears with its inspiring message about the power of love.*

> *Afterwards, I was crying in the parking lot, silently asking*
> *Spirit for direction towards my higher purpose.*
> *The tree in the island spoke to me audibly,*
> *crying out like me for freedom from the pavement containing it.*
> *It told me to let go and follow my heart.*

> *I drove to my favorite beach, walked to the water,*
> *stripped naked and let myself drift with the outgoing tide down the creek*
> *towards the ocean, face up, looking at the stars.*

> *In that moment, I let myself surrender to the power of the present*
> *and reconnected with the love that lives inside and all around me.*
> *I was completely present to myself and the world,*
> *identifying with the pure love that all things are made of.*

That was a profound experience for me. But you don't need to strip naked and jump in a creek to experience the power and freedom of that kind of love. Meditation is a simple practice that can do that for you, and it is the most effective way to practice paying attention to life. It is nice to have a special spot and a generous amount of time to do it. A sacred temple and a cool guru would be neat too. But remember, none of these things are necessary. You can meditate anywhere anytime for any duration. Even a few minutes stolen from a day filled with activity are valuable.

Find your posture. Focus on your breathing. Pay complete attention to whatever is happening in your life in this moment, and re-experience the love and oneness of life. There is no need to look elsewhere. You have everything you are looking for within you. Live today as if it is your last! Whenever you do this, you are remembering your true essence, and living in love.

About the Author

Jeff Thibodeau is the author of a personal growth guidebook entitled *Be Your Best! A Roadmap to Living a Healthy, Balanced and Fulfilling Life,* and a featured author in *Adventures in Manifesting Health and Happiness.*

Jeff is a natural therapeutic specialist, licensed massage therapist, cranial sacral/core synchronism therapist, and environmental planner and designer. He is also an experienced martial artist, fitness trainer, musician, teacher and speaker. He attended the New Mexico School of Natural Therapeutics and received a bachelor of science as well as a master's degree from Cornell University. He holds a black belt and instructor-certification in Shaolin kung fu.

Jeff's work and writing is inspired by his desire to live a healthy, balanced, and fulfilling life and to help others do the same.

http://www.jeffthibodeau.com

THE MAGICAL POTENTIAL OF TRUE LOVE

Marla Martenson

My whole life revolves around romance, dreams, and soul mates.

I marvel when the right biochemistry ignites sparks that become a flame so intense as to burn eternally; when two people embrace the magical potential of true love which becomes a forever-burning flame, lighting the course of their future. I am an artist and lovers are my palette, a modern day Picasso of sorts.

You see, I am a matchmaker.

People look to me every day to give them hope that, yes, they too can find their soul mate. My specialized knowledge, however, has been learned, in part, the hard way.

My first encounter with the illusion of true love occurred when I was a young, struggling actress in Hollywood. I had always felt very confident about myself in the looks department and was often asked for my autograph. I would sign it as *Molly Ringwald* and then add *just kidding*. Eyes shining with stars, body surging with hormones, I fell for an incredibly handsome, charismatic, and talented French chef, Bruno. He had deep-green eyes, full, pouty lips, and thick, chestnut brown hair that fell just above his shoulders in ringlets. I used to *love* stretching one out and letting it go.

I told my aunt one day, "I'm lucky to be with Bruno. I mean, it's amazing I was able to attract such a great-looking guy in the first place."

She looked at me like I'd lost my mind.

I pretty much had.

I had only known him for six adventure-filled months when we got married. I was smitten and, yes, I know: a heartbreak was imminent. But it wasn't just his looks I adored. Our wedding in his small village in France was a fairytale. We posed in the nearby woods where white cyclamen grew wild, and my white lace dress rose out of the blossoms; white against white. And the food! To Bruno and his wonderful family, food was a spiritual experience, savored and revered as an art form. What could possibly go wrong?

Unfortunately, I didn't realize that the bonfire of my true love needed more fuel than my attraction to a gorgeously chiseled face, a French accent, and his skill at preparing coquilles Saint Jacques. I was *in love*, and I thought I understood that the key to having true love in my life was to begin by loving myself. I was pretty sure that I did. But the way I allowed myself to be treated, suggested otherwise.

My beloved didn't think I was good enough the way I was.

In his opinion, I was an uptight ball-breaker with hair that was the wrong color; he wanted me to bleach it blonde. Teeth? Not white enough. Nails? Too short. Breasts? Too small. Skin color (yes, skin color!)? Too white. You'd think I resembled what could be best described as a red-headed albino frog with fangs.

I am pale and my skin burns easily. But Bruno bought me a gift certificate for several sessions at the local tanning salon and threatened to divorce me if I didn't get breast implants. My self-esteem imploded, simultaneously feeling awe of his overconfidence. What he used to do was look at himself in the mirror, as he was getting ready to go out, and declare, "God, I'm good-looking!" Then he would jump on his vintage motorcycle and speed off into the night, often not returning until the next day.

Even though I had lost my mind, I adored hanging out with the *Frenchies* as I used to call them. His French friends held garden parties in the evenings, stringing twinkle lights and playing international music. With cigarettes of tobacco or marijuana at their lips, they would talk of their international travels, their easy laughter filling the warm summer nights. I felt like I was in a new world; a secret club with a secret language that I quickly became fluent in. They were enlightening, exhilarating, carefree, and completely comfortable in their own skins – which I was trying to be. They lived in the moment. If they felt like making love, they could do so without getting attached. They did it for pure pleasure, something I hadn't quite been able to do. The casual way that the French viewed their bodies intrigued me. Men and women were never embarrassed to slip nude into a Jacuzzi together at a party. Women sunbathed topless all the time. It was completely natural to them.

Bruno would constantly saunter around the apartment *au naturel*. He went so far as to answer the door in his birthday suit. Frankly, I was appalled. His best friend James would knock on the door, and there came Bruno treating his buddy to a full frontal extravaganza and a big *bonjour*! James wasn't fazed in the least. One day Bruno shocked a pair of Jehovah's Witnesses.

"Aren't you embarrassed to have your privates on display?" I asked.

He gestured toward his package and shrugged his shoulders. *"C'est une partie du corps."* (English: It's just a part of the body.) *"You are so uptight, Marla."*

For all the French freedom, I watched girlfriends and wives as they discovered their young men cheating on them all the time. I couldn't figure out if they were just dumb, or if they had their own flings going on. I didn't think I would be able to recover from a betrayal.

But then it happened to me. I stayed with Bruno after he had an affair with James' sister who was visiting from France. My self-esteem hit rock bottom… or so I thought. Turned out: Things could get worse.

Much worse.

Bruno's green card came in the mail after we had been married for three years. What a coincidence that an hour after it arrived, he told me that he didn't want to be with me anymore. I was so distraught that I went up to Sunset Boulevard to a tattoo parlor, blaring Guns and Roses as I drove. I chose to subject myself to modern day torture by having a tattoo engraved on my left hip: a heart with a dagger through it with the words, *l'amour*.

I was a mess!

I couldn't eat or sleep and my heart literally felt as though it had been pierced by a dagger. I was able to convince Bruno to stay with me after that, but why did I want to hang on to someone who didn't love me? I tried changing my personality to be *more cool* and *easygoing*. When he was there with his friends, I even walked around the house as nonchalant as a cigarette dangling from my lips could make me. All I got was a sore throat.

After four more years of tears and anguish, we finally parted for good. I packed two suitcases, took my three-pound Yorkshire terrier, and moved to Chicago where I had some wonderful friends waiting to uplift and support me.

At first I cried at the sound of a motorcycle, or when I would see his favorite yogurt at the super market, but within a couple of months, I had pretty much exorcized him. And that felt wonderful!

My energy lifted, my self-esteem was slowly climbing, and amazing things started happening for me. I signed with a commercial agent and booked two commercials in one week. As much as I'd like to blame Bruno for everything, to be fair, I always had the choice to leave, so my unhappiness was of my own making.

I needed to find the meaning of true self-love to pave the way for lasting love with a soul mate.

Yet, I think there was another angle to my sojourn with Bruno. Maybe in life's journey we need the very people that we love to force us to grow. I mean, I thought I was fine, but Bruno uncovered my weak spot and used it for target practice. And even though I thought my self-image was good, it wasn't all it needed to be, so I attracted someone that showed me exactly what I needed to work on.

I couldn't really *see myself*, and so I couldn't really *see* Bruno. Other people are mirrors, and our own reflection in their eyes isn't always rosy, but it may be useful.

I delved into self-help books, and began a strong spiritual practice of reflection and meditation. For a while, I still picked the wrong guys along the way, but my interest fizzled quickly. Then some magic began to happen for me and hasn't stopped ever since.

One particularly warm spring evening in 2001, after my father passed away, I walked to a pharmacy up on Sunset Boulevard in Hollywood to get some vitamins. There I met a delightful petite Polish woman from New York who also lived in the neighborhood and managed an apartment building, called Sabrina. We became solid friends and went to plays and comedy clubs together. Sabrina was always talking about a guy who lived in her building. Adolfo. She told me he was dating a gal, but it wasn't serious.

I didn't really care to hear about a guy who was already in a relationship, but every time I saw Sabrina, she kept talking about this guy. She told me that he played piano at a place in Playa Del Rey. I can't explain it, but I felt like my dad was nudging me. I was just kind of glowing with expectation of the night I decided to go to the piano bar with Sabrina to secretly check him out.

I liked his music; the way he played the piano, and just… the way he looked. He was a handsome Latino with a warm smile. He came over and sat with us on his break and after he finished playing that night, we all went over to Sabrina's apartment, sat next to each other on the couch, and drank some cognac. When Sabrina left the room to get something, our fingers touched and then… our lips. I don't know, they just somehow … locked like magnets.

This man saw me with the eyes of love. My beauty took his breath away and he wrote a song for me that was later used on TV. We got married in a charming five-hundred-year-old church in Mexico City. My simple yet elegant gown slightly blushed a pink so pale it was almost white, and silk roses clustered just at my lower back. It rained at the end of our reception, which I was told meant good luck – which has proven true.

I had finally found my true love. My soul mate.

A few years after we were married, Adolfo walked up to me in the living room and said, "I have a message for you. God told me to tell you to write. Forget about acting. You need to write."

"But I don't want to forget about acting," I replied, totally confused.

"Well, I got the message, so you'd better follow up on it," he said as he turned and walked back into his studio.

My head was spinning. Adolfo had no idea about my lifelong dream of becoming a published author. It was something that had beckoned to me my whole life and I'd dabbled, but never felt confident or talented enough to pursue seriously. I had been working as a matchmaker for a few years and had a lot of advice and entertaining tales to tell. The thought of writing a dating book had crossed my mind. "I will go for it!" I decided right then and there.

Thank you, mi amor.

When you see each other through the eyes of true love, you see who you both really are, and you nurture the dreams each one holds. So, as lovers, we must not only love what we see, but we must also truly see the one we love.

About the Author

Marla is the dating expert in the land of beautiful people. Early in her career, she turned her talent into a full-time profession, helping the rich and famous find their soul mates.

Marla is the author of several books including *Excuse Me, Your Soul Mate Is Waiting*, and has been interviewed on the Today Show, WGN Chicago Morning News, San Diego Living, Urban Rush, CTV Calgary, Better TV, KUSI San Diego Morning Show, and over fifty radio shows including Coast to Coast AM with George Noory and The Cooper Lawrence Show.

Marla and her husband reside in Los Angeles, where she continues to bring her considerable matchmaking expertise to the singles of star-studded Southern California.

http://www.cupidforhire.com

http://www.marlamartenson.com

SEND ME A SHOOTING STAR

David Saywell

In the quiet moments I spend with my wife, I often wonder if we'd met many years ago, either as infants or toddlers when we lived in the same small town.

Some fourteen years after our births, our paths crossed when I returned to live in the same town again and a few years later we again returned to each other's lives, only this time never to leave.

In a way the journey feels very similar to a planet passing inside and outside the orbit of another, each on their own cosmic journey; should their journeys become one we would find ourselves contemplating an entirely new and different reality. And, here I am.

And here we are!

I could never have possibly imagined that we'd be here, now, leading such a charmed life with three beautiful children, living our dreams, being so connected. Holding each other in the warmest of embraces, our eyes catch the gaze of the other and there they remain lost in the dream-inspired awe of the other; dancing, playing, kissing. All in a single breath and in the next saying *I love you* and meaning it with every eternal fiber of our being in that timeless moment.

Our dreams are never done. They are constantly evolving in harmony with the new creations we bring into our lives. The one constant we both share is an eternal dream of love; for each other, for life, for our family, and for the dream itself.

Here's our dream with verses taken from my journal along the way:

Before the beginning...

It rose above and disappeared
My life with you had just appeared.
Send me a shooting star
You're the love of my life; I hope you know you are.

It might have been an epiphany or premonition, in which during a moment of clarity I saw and felt our lives together. At the time I didn't know who the love of my life was but I knew she was out there and I knew that our life together would be amazing.

When we finally made the transition from knowing each other to becoming friends to becoming lovers, the experience was intoxicating!

After one month...

"One for one
Won't you come?
Lamplight love as we talk,
Together, on this moonlight walk."

Love was there, growing between us, we knew very early on that we had something special. By month three we were both head over heels in love, spending more and more time together, hours outside in the cold; till the early hours of the morning saying goodbye and daydreaming of our next encounter, romantic surprises, fun weekend getaways and feelings for each other we'd never felt before.

After twelve months...

Who would have thought that you'd be the one so many years ago?
This past year has shown me and I've grown to know.
That, for the magic in your eyes and the tenderness in your touch,
I love you, so very much.

We've grown closer day after day.
I'd like to be closer again, if you may.
So come and join me, in this bright eyed diamond life.
With this ring, I ask you to be my wife.

A proposal on the anniversary of our first year together as a couple!

We'd shared so many experiences in our short time together, grown to know each other so intimately, spent countless moments absolutely infatuated with each other, and dreaming of what the future would hold. We both knew we wanted to spend the rest of our lives together. And this... was just the beginning.

For now and evermore...

Hope is a passionate dream,
Of the life and love we wish to see.
Dream a dream and fantasize,
An' you shall find some sweet surprise.

To this day we live passionately, in hopeful expectation and constant dreaming, knowing that when we dream together we can effortlessly create anything we desire. Inevitably we're always surprised at what turns up!

Over the last fifteen years since we began our lives together, I've observed love in its most beautifully powerful forms. I've seen and felt how it relates to others, the Universe, and me.

When you truly love someone they shine like a star...

When the sun does shine
And stars align,
Thoughts are right
And love takes flight
Above the trees, over the hills,
Colliding with the sun
And with sprinkling stars my heart does fill.

Pour heartfelt-love onto anyone and they will become more beautiful with each passing moment. Look deeply into their eyes and you'll know it instantly. Sustain that connection for more than a glance and you'll feel it. Bring it to life with a dreamy gaze that will feel like an eternity! It's a beautiful and powerful connection with the energy that creates worlds; a heart to heart connection through the windows of our eyes.

**When you truly love something it becomes
one of the most beautiful things in your universe...**

*Sweet butterflies
Dance in her eyes,
Preserving an element of soft surprise
That an angel's heart cannot surmise.*

As with another person, the relationship between us and absolutely anything else is profoundly affected by love.

It's the difference between a tree being just a tree and a magnificent living being eternally part of the sacred ecology of the earth. Or the difference between the night sky being a thick blanket of darkness or a starry source of wonder and inspiration. It's the difference between a pair of swans and their cygnets in a picture, swimming on a lake, and an emotional realization of the power of creation and beauty in this world.

The world around us is just that. But it can be so much more, depending on your perspective and the amount of love you allow to flow through the wonder in your gaze; tapping into the essence of who you really are and allowing the full creativity to flow through into these profoundly meaningful moments.

When you truly love yourself the most amazing thing occurs...

*I closed my eyes, and rose above...
My heart was filled with unconditional Love.*

If magic does exist, it's certain to be found in that intrinsic relationship between true love and self love; each one nurturing the other with a Universal connection running so deep within us that this very difference could only be felt with our hearts. To know one is to know the other, and when you accept them both as one and allow them to manifest in your experience, they shall set you free.

In every moment we are manifesting our experience. Manifestation surrounds us; it's the way we feel as we move through our day, observing the creations around us, the people we meet, and the way we interact. Our lives are unfolding one manifestation after the other. If we can be present in the moment, aware of the manifestation that's happening now, we gain control of our experience and what we manifest. We can choose how we feel and love in any moment; to feel good, we can allow ourselves to love and be loved. These pure positive emotions are ultimate manifestations and the Source of all others.

This life is such a sensuous experience. We are all loved and when we know, feel, and radiate how much we are loved, we get to experience the full spectrum of what it means to be here.

And it feels good.

About the Author

David Saywell is an author, poet and speaker with a self-described *unique take on life*. He writes and speaks on topics related to personal and spiritual development.

David has a heartfelt desire to share his experiences and work at the leading edge of creation in the New Earth, inspiring others to do the same.

Following an intense and spiritual six-month odyssey through some of the most remote parts of Australia, David now resides in a small country town, north of Melbourne.

Live the full expression of your soul's desire… now! There are no limits. This is just the beginning.

http://www.davidsaywell.com

CROSSING THE RIVER

Pollyanna Darling

In the *Hero's Journey,* Joseph Campbell quotes his friend Heinrich Zimmer: "... the radio station WOB, Wisdom of the Buddha, is broadcasting all the time. But you've got to have a receiving set. And until you have the receiving set, well, you're not getting the message."

He continues: "You can't teach Buddhism, you can't teach illumination. You can give different clues to how to get it. But if a person isn't willing to paddle his own canoe, he's not going to get across the river."

So it is with love.

Broadcasting

On a balmy December night, I swept into the party wrapped in emerald sequins and shimmering gold body-paint. Filled with a renewed energy and love for life, I intended to laugh, dance, and spend time with my friends. Not long before, I had left a marriage of twelve years; a step that was painful yet liberating. I relished my freedom and the opportunity to spend time just being me. My three children were with their father for the weekend and I was ready to kick up my heels.

I certainly hadn't planned to meet my soul partner.

After a year of deep personal development and intensive intuitive training, I was clear on the direction I wanted to take for the first time in my life. Although I had received intuitive guidance that what I truly wanted was a passionate, loving relationship with a beautiful man, I dismissed it as being a long way off. My sensible, practical, rational, critical head told me that no one would want me anyway.

Why would anyone want a thirty-five year-old single mother with no money and crazy ideas?

As everyone relaxed into the evening, I felt my high spirits waning a little. I chatted with a couple of friends, when someone behind me said, "Hello."

I spun around laughing. There before me, stood a tall, lithe, curly-haired, rather scruffy but quite handsome man. His blue eyes twinkled and as I met his gaze, I distinctly heard a quiet voice somewhere in my consciousness say, "Oh, it's you!" I was looking into the face of a stranger who I recognized with absolute certainty. The whole world vanished, time faltered and stopped.

All that existed in that moment was the space between us: a chasm filled with electric energy.

Later, tucked away from the rest of the party, teasing each other, laughing, and swapping stories, I couldn't quite bring myself to look Asher in the eye. When he shyly suggested I go home with him, I remembered my earlier guidance to surrender to this man and allow the flow.

So, utterly out of my comfort zone… I agreed.

In the darkness, we made our way through the trees to the star-lit beach, Asher moving branches from my path, holding my arm gently as I stepped onto the sand. As we kissed with the water moving at our feet, I leant into his warm body. Bliss!

Suddenly self-conscious and uncomfortable, I asked a question to fill the silence. "When were you born?"

"Nineteen eighty—"

I froze. Anyone born in nineteen eighty-anything was too young.

I freaked out. What was I doing frolicking on the beach with a baby? How ridiculous and embarrassing! What on earth would this young, single chap think if he knew my whole story? I tried flinging a few facts at him in the hope he'd disappear.

Asher wasn't fazed.

In fact, he seemed to find my discomfort amusing and he kissed me again. I told myself we were just two people kissing on a beach, no big deal and renewed my resolve to allow the evening to unfold naturally.

Asher and I wandered along the darkened beach, sang in the playground, and laid in the still sun-warm, musky dirt on our backs. We cruised the streets, hands entwined and eventually snuck into his room, lowering our voices so as not to wake house-mates.

By then, my gold body-paint was crisp and tight. I felt like a lizard that had outgrown its skin. Asher asked me if I'd like him to remove it. At my hesitant nod he disappeared, returning with armfuls of steaming towels. As he smoothed the cracked paint from my tired body, I surrendered to one of the most blissful, innocent, and intimate experiences of my entire life.

Not Getting The Message

So began six months of not getting the message. Clouded by doubt and unpleasant thoughts about myself, I avoided this man, though I recognized him deep in my soul.

I was often hijacked by my beliefs and assumptions, unleashed from unconscious depths by the possibility of love. In moments of doubt, I defined myself as a predator, ridiculous and a drab mother who was too old and too far away.

You can't begin another relationship so soon after your marriage ends. You'll ruin his life. He doesn't want to take on three children that aren't his own! You're too old and you'll have nothing in common, so why would he want you?

On and on it went.

My thoughts were driven by unconscious beliefs made up during my childhood in response to not having my needs fully met. Naming them was a large part of staying sane. *I'm unlovable, I can't trust men, and I can't have what I want.* I did my best to be as cool as a cucumber - uncommitted, uninspiring, and evasive.

To my great surprise (and secret delight) Asher pursued me with fervor, texting, calling, and making it abundantly clear that he wasn't going to give up.

During this time, I repeatedly used my intuitive skills to receive guidance on my true path and what to do about our developing relationship. Time and again, I was told to flow with what was unfolding, to trust my heart, and to stay with it. I followed this counsel to the best of my ability, allowing my doubts and dark thoughts to exist, but acting on what I knew to be true.

It was a strange and wild time.

Despite my attempts to derail the process, our connection deepened, and we spent hours on the phone. I *loved* the rich, resonant sound of his voice. My children immediately liked Asher and he liked them. Our delicious, blissful, and extraordinary lovemaking was out of this world. In that union that I experienced magical connection on every level: physical, emotional, etheric, and spiritual.

The random young man I met at a party revealed himself to be thoughtful, interesting, gentle, loving, strong, fun, quirky, intelligent, creative, and deeply sexy.

Everything I would never admit to wanting!

The Receiving Set

I loved spending time with Asher. As the year progressed, the doubting inner voices began to wane. They diminished from a raucous crowd to a gaggle and then to a couple of dissenters with placards. The more action I took from my intuition, the more I trusted the voice of my heart and the more beauty, magic, and love flowed into my life. It seemed like I had at last found the ability to receive.

Accompanied by my familiar, but much quieter, sense of trepidation, Asher and I created a home together. Everything flowed with ease and grace. We were supported by friends and family as we very deliberately created a vision of what we would love in our lives, taking action towards that.

I had intuitively known for a few years that I would have another child, but had no idea how that would eventuate. It seemed like the perfect time: I was with a lovely man who had no children of his own and my three were older, so why not? Asher didn't appear quite as enthusiastic as me, but we both used our own processes to discover the truth and so agreed that a baby would be a grand creation.

To my delight, I became pregnant almost immediately. I was sure it was a girl but didn't want to think too much about it until we were sure. The first signs of trouble began about five weeks into the pregnancy, when I had mild, niggling cramps and felt odd. One cool autumn morning, as I hung up the phone on a dreadful radio interview, I doubled over as a radiating, stabbing pain gnawed at my belly. I crawled to the couch and used the most reliable tool I have: my intuition.

I let go of any need to know and imaginatively stepped into the pain. In my mind's eye, I clearly saw a torn fallopian tube.

Throughout the ensuing hours, Asher was by my side. In agony and with a disturbing sensation that something was really wrong, I was rushed to the hospital's emergency department. An ectopic pregnancy can be difficult to diagnose, but I knew what I had seen and told the doctors. A few raised eyebrows suggested I was imagining things, but a blood test confirmed my story.

Drifting in and out, under white sheets and glaring lights, I could see Asher in a chair next to me. Slowly, the awful sensation that there was something terribly wrong began to fade. I felt myself drawing back, receding into a great expansive light that embraced me as I softened into it. My attachments to this world – my children, Asher, everything that mattered – melted away as I gave myself to the light, held in the energy of all that is.

Suddenly, a voice jolted me back into the glaring fluorescent, bleeping cubicle. "Pollyanna!" It was Asher, calling me back from the very edge of life.

Shortly afterwards, I had an emergency surgery – the fetus had implanted itself in my fallopian tube instead of the uterus. My tube had ruptured and I was bleeding into my pelvic cavity. Without swift medical intervention, I would have died. As it was, I lost the tube and the fetus.

In the following weeks, as I sobbed out my grief and shock, it was Asher who wordlessly held me, cared for me, and supported me in healing.

The last of my resistance melted away.

Crossing the River

After this, we began making a conscious choice to create our *love-child*; a living expression of our connection. I only had one tube and my chances of falling pregnant were halved, but I knew that with the power of my consciousness in my heart, we could create almost anything. Although I was a little afraid of having another ectopic pregnancy, I once again chose not to succumb to my fear. It remained, but I took action toward my truth.

Asher and I began planning a wedding, a celebration of our love and connection. One overcast, windy morning we invited our friends to join us at dawn on a seawall. Everyone wore white and the rays of the sun pierced the clouds as we said our vows, lighting up our faces. Even the wind eased to hear our words of love. It was a dreamy, magical day, made more enchanting by the presence of a growing babe in my belly.

A little over a year after my near-death experience, our son was born: chubby, happy, strong, and beautiful: our love-child. The radiant, life-affirming little chap he is completes our blended family.

Had I listened to the doubting voices and taken the action they urged me to take – to abandon my relationship with Asher – I would have neither the deep, abiding love and connection I share with my man, nor the child who brings me (and everyone around him) so much joy. Using, following, and trusting my intuition, even when my rational self is writhing in discomfort, has brought me love, magic and, most importantly, a life I never even imagined.

Crossing the river takes vision, courage, and action in favor of what you would love to create.

Nothing that your heart truly desires is impossible.

About the Author

Pollyanna is the author of *The Relationship Revelation*, an experienced intuitive life coach, speaker, poet, singer, blogger, and mother of four boys. She is passionate about inspiring and empowering others to create more love in their lives. Pollyanna loves to write – to share knowledge, to inspire, to tell untold stories, for travel to imaginative realms and just for the sheer, unbridled joy of it! She has a natural intuitive gift that brings wisdom, humor, and guidance to both herself and everyone who asks for it.

Pollyanna exudes a beauty and passion that is a wonderful exotic blend of feminine power and optimism that makes anything seem possible. She has a deep and energizing connection to the natural world and laughs loudly and often!

http://www.pollyannadarling.com

SELF-LOVE: WOULD IT CHANGE ANYTHING? OR EVERYTHING?

Michelle Marie McGrath

My path of self-love started out in a very ordinary way. It was at a time in my life when I was feeling lost. Frustrated with my job and confused in my marriage, I was bored with myself.

Was this it?

I knew there was more to life than that, but I had no idea where to start. It felt like I had taken a wrong turn somewhere but there were no directions. Whatever I did just seemed to bring up more questions in me. And the more I tried to understand what was going on, the more confused I felt.

What Do I Need Most?

One night I was meditating and feeling sorry for myself. I took a deep breath and said, "Ok what is it? What's wrong with me? What is it that I need most?" The clear response was: *self-love*. I had to admit that yes I did have self-esteem issues, but didn't everyone?

Great. Now what?

Immediately what came to mind is the often suggested exercise of staring into your own eyes in the mirror, slapping on a big toothy grin and saying, 'I love you. Yeah you baby.'

This felt impossible. Surely there was more to it than this.

I continued meditating and I saw the image of a bottle with lots of ingredients flying into it creating a self-love oil. I created the oil and meditated with it each night for a couple of months, setting a specific intention to release blockages to self-love whilst I slept. Months of crazy dreams followed whereby I would wake up with insights into where and why I was holding myself back.

Something was shifting inside me.

It was unpleasant to start noticing my role in dysfunctional patterns that were playing out. Although I became increasingly aware of unconscious beliefs that were creating my dissatisfaction, it felt like I was barely scratching the surface.

What Would 100% Self-Love Look Like?

In my frustration, I felt compelled to tell the Universe that I wanted to let go of *everything* that was standing in the way of 100% self-love. Not just a bit: 100%, thank you very much with a cherry on top. I did not truly understand the implications of that intention. A jumble of mixed emotions started to bubble up to the surface, along with painful feelings that I was not used to acknowledging. This became increasingly confronting as I admitted to myself that I was really unhappy and felt trapped.

Seven years prior, when I was twenty-five, I had moved to Australia to get married and was now living on the other side of the world, away from my family and close friends. Maybe this fairytale romance was not going to have a happy ending after all. Surely all long-term relationships go through challenging times. Then, when a couple more years of denial passed by, while we continued to ignore a herd of elephants crowding the room, I gradually admitted I was living a lie. It was gradual because it had taken years to be honest with myself about my situation. Finally, I stopped hoping things would change. I realized it was time to stop trying to *fix* things and that *I could only change myself.*

Yet I still failed to take action.

The Universe is Always Responding

It was New Year's Eve. Reflecting on the year gone by, I looked up at the stars and stated to the Universe, 'This year I want everything that is not in alignment with my highest truth to be dissolved.'

I was surprised I didn't hear hysterical laughter coming from the heavens.

Fast-forward a couple of months: I was suddenly tired all the time, weak and nauseous. Having children was something I had a resistance toward. Later, what seemed completely obvious to me, was that a part of me knew it would not be right for us to create a family.

It felt surreal but I was pregnant. However, I knew a baby would not eventuate.

During this time I was working at home in my natural therapies practice. I was in such turmoil and felt as though I was observing my life play out from a distance. The neighbors living a floor below decided to renovate and started knocking walls down. Each time I was about to start a session with a client, the jackhammers began. My foundations were literally being demolished beneath me.

It came as no surprise to me to discover the fetus had no heartbeat. On the way to the scan I told my husband with certainty, "This is not going to happen."

He stared at me in stunned silence.

There were complications with my miscarriage linked to a pregnancy-related cancer. I was the wrong age, ethnic background, and socio-economic group, and so the doctors found it fascinating. How could I say "there's a big karmic release going on here and this is a catalyst to end this relationship" without sounding unhinged?

I knew the Universe was leading me somewhere else, not that I had any idea where that may be. I was sent for a chest X-ray immediately to see if the cells had spread into my lungs and if I needed chemotherapy.

Two weeks later, my husband moved out.

After eleven years together, our relationship ended as abruptly as it had begun.

You May be Forced to Change Direction

Next I had my driving license suspended due to a temporary speed change that I had somehow failed to notice. With nowhere to live, no assets, no family in the country, no money, and no fit-state to work, this was a very challenging time.

How did I get here?

It was a chilling realization to grasp how rapidly people can become homeless due to a sudden change in circumstances. I could barely eat or sleep. I dropped two clothes sizes in a month. My life was crumbling around me and I felt as though I was disappearing. A little voice inside me said, "This is what you asked for."

This was not the vision of where I wanted to be at thirty-five.

Strangely, it felt inevitable. I started to wonder if I had swapped lives with an actress on a daytime soap working with a badly written script.

When You Take Too Long to Make a Decision The Universe Will Make it For You

The Universe stepped in with a friend who needed a house-sitter for six weeks. A few loyal, saintly friends were tirelessly patient as they listened to my tortured ranting. I reeled and staggered through my days for months. I felt sucked dry by the onslaught of feelings of shock, humiliation, betrayal, and disbelief that this was how my life was playing out.

If this was all for the best, then why did it hurt so much?

I regularly found myself staring at dog food or other obscure items in the supermarket with tears streaming down my cheeks, unable to remember why I was there.

When did I become so familiar with this heavy, throbbing pain in my chest?

Sometimes Everything Has to Fall Apart so it Can Fall Into Place

Betrayal can come in many forms. Self-betrayal is surely the most hurtful. The greatest betrayal that we can experience comes in the way we ignore our inner wisdom and by doing so, we deny ourselves. There is nothing more painful than ignoring the whispers of our own hearts.

How often do we deny that gentle voice inside of us?

Sometimes the only thing that dramatically attracts our attention and makes us stop is when this pattern is reflected back to us by the person closest to us. Our illusions are shattered. No place left to hide.

The next few years were a blur of depression, insomnia, and confusion, seeking answers from everywhere and everyone else except from myself. I moved through my days on autopilot, feeling invisible. I took myself to Brazil for a retreat. My intended two-month stay of meditation and deep inner work stretched into almost seven. I felt so debilitated that I questioned the validity of my life.

What use am I to anyone?

There seemed to be no point to anything and I was taking up unnecessary space. Unsurprisingly, I continued attracting situations and people that reinforced how deeply betrayed, rejected, unappealing, and unattractive I felt. I was manifesting external situations that mirrored perfectly what I was feeling on the inside.

Choose to Love the Unlovable

I repeatedly restated my commitment to 100% self-love and journeyed into the most confronting and painful parts of me. I felt like I was drowning in unfamiliar emotions, such as jealousy, resentment, rage, and self-loathing, and I became intimately acquainted with all of them. What I discovered were raw and vulnerable parts of me, starved of my attention. Realizations were deep and shocking as I encountered my levels of self-rejection. My own body felt like a foreign object.

How could I ever hope to have an intimate, meaningful, loving relationship with anyone if I was so unwilling to love me?

I was learning to open my heart to me. At last!

Even though these experiences were painful, I was so aware that each step had brought me to this exact point in my life. I finally felt nothing but gratitude for my ex-husband because his actions forced me into a deeper exploration of myself. It was a chance to start my life afresh.

How could I possibly feel any regret?

After all, other people in our lives are merely catalysts.

Divorce And Depression Are Opportunities For Transformation

How we feel about ourselves is *never* about anyone else. Transformation occurs when we can allow feelings to arise without judging them. When we learn compassion for ourselves no matter what we are experiencing, there is nothing to reject or deny. This can be difficult to accept because it means self-responsibility. When we stop projecting our needs onto everyone else, the buck stops here. Nobody else can fulfill any desire within us. Yes they can share in our happiness, but only when we have found the love *within* ourselves.

We Create Our Own Lives in Every Moment

We are all amazing at manifestation. When we do not love ourselves enough to make empowering choices and create healthy boundaries, other people and the Universe will make these decisions for us. I have learnt that saying *no* to others can mean saying *yes* to me. Unhealthy relationships have naturally fallen away. This act of self-love has created a space that is now increasingly filled with inspiring and authentic people.

By sending out an intention into the Universe, we set things into motion.

Here's the tricky part: We have no idea what that will look like. One of the most challenging things to let go of is our self-perception. Yet when we do, it creates space for something new and profoundly different to be created.

Are you open to this possibility of allowing the most empowered version of you to step forward?

Fill Yourself With Love and Allow It to Overflow

So where am I now? In a place of inner peace and treating myself like my own best friend. This commitment has also evolved into a love-filled business, creating gorgeous products that remind others to fall in love with themselves every day.

It has been completely true for me: *you teach what you most need to learn*.

Once we take ownership for giving ourselves the love we desire, it is externally reflected back to us. I experience this every day. Doors are opening magically due to the magnetic force of my self-love.

When we welcome and acknowledge everything about ourselves that we find difficult to accept, what is left?

Self-love.

What would your life look like if you invited 100% self-love to play the leading role?

Think about it.

About the Author

Michelle Marie McGrath is the chief self-lover of Sacred Self and creates a Divine self-love range of Alchemical oils and cards. She is passionate about falling in love with all parts of herself. Originally from the UK, Michelle currently lives in Sydney, Australia where she explores her favorite self-loving activities: soaking in the bath; meditating with crystals; escaping into a gripping novel; beeswax candles; buying herself flowers; New Zealand Sauvignon Blanc; lying in bed listening to the rain; massages; chai tea; organic chocolate; eating raspberries; watching sunsets; stand-up comedy and travelling to sacred sites. Her idea of bliss is a simultaneous combination of all these activities!

Michelle believes that our most challenging experiences can transform into the most magical gifts. She is learning to embrace vulnerability and explore the freedom behind it. It is a dream come true to share her heart-made products around the world and be an ambassador for self-love.

http://www.sacredself.com.au

11:11 LOVE STORY

John & Kathy Stringer

Our story begins before this time, this place, this form; in a time where all is one and we were extensions joined as twin flames and sent into incarnations to experience life in many ways. At least, that is our understanding. It is this form, this time, this life experience, and this perspective *when* we chose to reunite.

So, our story in this form begins with typical births and upbringings that exposed us each to somewhat different paths; similar enough to create common ground and common desires, yet different enough for our union to create the balance we desired.

Kathy: From the moment I first met John Stringer in 11/1996, seven years before we fell in love, I recognized his humble and honest spirit. When I thought of, or saw, him I always thought, "He is a good man." Though I realized he was a very special person, I didn't really know, or feel in any way attracted to, him because, at the time, I was deeply in love with my husband. We met at a music venue where he was in a singing competition against my then boyfriend (soon to be husband), Jeffrey. Although Jeffrey won the singing competition, John and I started on an amazing journey that would lead us to love like we have never known.

Over the next seven years, John popped up in my life in many synchronistic ways. He would send e-mails as a fan of (my then husband) Jeffrey's music about song inspiration, not knowing that I, as Jeffrey's manager, answered his emails. He came out to Jeffrey's shows and I would always see that there was something positive and honest about him. When speaking to him, it felt as if I was present with him and I would let go of my concerns and worries. I know now that John was my twin flame awaiting the right time to reunite with me as my one true love.

John: I grew up in a family with a loving sister and a nurturing mother and an absent father. My mother often taught me about relating to women and the importance of *the little things*. And though I didn't exactly understand then, I suspect she played a part in my becoming an idealistic romantic at a very early age.

After my first long-term girlfriend was unfaithful while I was away in college, I chose to stop trusting women and feared getting too close. I decided that if I wasn't clear at a certain point in the relationship, usually around the sixth month, I'd move on. Eventually, I began dating in open relationships; a style I first learned in college. Yet, all of those relationships ended unfavorably.

Kathy: In July of 2002 I learned my husband, who I loved so much and I was so sure loved me the same, was having an affair. After 11 years together as best friends, we were seen as the couple others wanted to be like. I was so grateful to have him in my life and thought we were so special. After the affair, I began to see that Jeffrey was not who I thought he was, and that I had lost sight of who I was.

On the road to divorce, I was filled with anger, hurt, and sorrow, but I made the decision to rediscover who I was and intended to become a better person on the other side of divorce. Although this was certainly one of the most challenging times in my life, I am so grateful for the journey that allowed me to trust myself and know that I deserve honest and genuine love.

I was blessed to go with my one and a half year-old daughter, Jolie, to Florida for a couple months to stay with my sister and be near my family while I put my life back together. A big turning point in my life occurred when I made a trip to my Aunt and Uncle's farm in Pittsboro, North Carolina, for Thanksgiving (11/2002).

While on the farm, I took long walks in nature and spent a lot of time in the hot tub looking up at the stars, watching hawks flying above me during the day, and reading an amazing book called *Gift of the Red Bird* by Paula D'arcy. These experiences allowed me to connect to God in a way I never knew possible. Once I left the farm, I not only quit smoking after ten years, but I felt at peace and real gratitude for all the blessings in my life.

I now consider this trip my spiritual awakening.

I came home to Atlanta with new hope and excitement about what life would bring next. I got still and wrote a list of what I truly felt I wanted in a soul mate. I recognized that the most important things to me in a partner would be honesty and selflessness. After I wrote it, I just put it away and remained grateful for where I was. I was fine with being on my own to focus on myself and my daughter.

John: Looking back, I see all the relationships leading up to finding Kathy as gifts to help me experience what I needed to gain clarity. I got so tired of experiencing unfavorable, volatile, and uncertain relationships that I decided to get clear about what I wanted.

One night, I first wrote down all the things I liked about past relationships and all the things I didn't. I then took the list of dislikes and wrote down the opposites to create a master list of what was important to me. Before that night, I would have told you about my ideal woman by describing physical attributes, but that night's list contained only qualities and values like loyalty, emotional stability, child-like nature, intelligence, business savvy, and being *addiction free*.

After reviewing my list and still feeling somewhat discouraged, the romantic idealist from childhood came barreling to the forefront and I felt a deep yearning for the magical connection I always believed in; one where bells rang and I'd recognize in a single moment who the right one would be because her soul would speak to me.

7-11 Our Magical Night

Kathy: John and I saw each other coming down the stairs of this packed club and I remember feeling so great about seeing him, like reuniting with an old friend. We spoke for what seemed like hours but his friends kept badgering him to leave and he finally gave in and decided to go. As he walked away, I felt sad, but hopeful, and said under my breath, "I wish I could dance with him." My friend heard my wish and ran after him to put into motion what would change my life forever.

She stopped this man whom she did not know and convinced him to come dance with me. As I saw him coming toward me, my heart leapt and he asked me to dance. We instantly wrapped our bodies around each other and just swayed to the music.

As we held each other, time stood still. My body, soul, and spirit were completely present and without fear. We danced in the middle of that floor holding each other like our lives depended on it. As the dance music pumped, I let go of all thoughts of *what will people think* and *what will come of this*, connecting with this man who was so clearly not what I thought was best for me then.

I closed my eyes and became one with another person like I had never known in my life, trusting the moment and that which led us there, and letting go of worries and concerns that allowed me to feel complete and utter bliss. I knew in that moment that I could have true and honest love after the pain of divorce.

John: It wasn't long before I connected with Kathy at a nightclub called 1150. We'd talked many times before and had great conversations, but given our history as friends and my typical dating style, I hadn't considered her in my quest to find *the one*.

After we both had a great conversation, I was leaving the club and her friend suggested I dance with Kathy before I left. Her friend countered my resistance by offering to take me to the after-party my friends and I were headed to, so I walked to the dance floor where I thought Kathy was dancing with another guy and the floor seemed to part like the red sea. The next thing I knew, Kathy and I were dancing, swept up into a moment of pure magic; a chemistry like I'd never felt before. It seemed everything else disappeared and all that mattered was our embrace in that single moment.

We danced that way and didn't realize that the music had stopped until the lights turned on and the staff was already sweeping the floor. Kathy and I were the last to leave.

What was equally amazing is that I had just written my list three days prior and the *magic* I'd hoped for had happened. After our dance, as Kathy and I walked off the dance floor, I couldn't help but wonder what had just happened, feeling more confused than certain. My mind kept thinking, "This couldn't be happening" because she was a music-conference manager who just ended a marriage and I was a musician still trying to figure life out.

And suddenly... boom!

We were swept up in the best chemistry I'd ever felt. Fortunately, that was just the beginning.

Kathy: After that night at 1150, we emailed each other for a couple of weeks and spoke on the phone. When we saw each other again, we both decided to throw caution to the wind and follow our hearts into a passionate relationship with each other.

The first few weeks were amazing in every way. I was so clear that we were supposed to be together and I assumed we would only see each other from here on out. Imagine my surprise when John was very honest with me in saying that he just wasn't ready to stop *seeing other people*. My heart sank but I agreed as I did not want to lose him. That night, I did a lot of soul searching and it became clear to me that I simply could not be with him if he was going to continue to be with others. By telling him my truth, I was willing to risk losing him to stay connected to the *self* I had rediscovered through my divorce.

John was shocked when I called and explained why I changed my mind. I found him to be honest in his response of just not being willing to stop seeing other women. I appreciated his honesty and we spent the next two weeks together as friends continuing to fall deeper in love. I will never forget the day he looked in my eyes and said, "You are all I want and I don't want to see anyone else." He also confessed that he had not been with anyone else but me since we started seeing each other.

I was so relieved.

As of this writing, we have been together for nine years, and since 11 has been such a frequent number in our lives (more then we have room to explain), we married on 11/11/2007; a day filled with love for us and all who attended.

We can truly say our marriage has been a catalyst in our ongoing spiritual growth. Communicating honestly and being vulnerable has allowed us to trust each other and, most importantly, trust in life itself.

About the Authors

John and Kathy Stringer are partners in life that have come together to help each other and to inspire others. Their desire for a life of balance and strong ties to family have helped them find a mutually rewarding life together and they continue to expand. They've grown, loved, and expanded together in so many ways, and are so grateful to have each other as soul partners in this journey. The *magic* has continued as life unfolds for them, step by step, ever so gently bringing them what they need and allowing them to let go of all they don't.

Whether you seek to find your twin flame, soul mate, or whomever, does not matter. What matters is the experience you choose in this lifetime. To experience love, caring for others, and growing to be that which you came to be: that's the ticket!

http://www.johnstringerinc.com

RELEASING YOUR PAST

Janelle McArthur

Being labeled as someone coming from a background of molestation, becoming a young teen mother, experiencing an abusive relationship, and being diagnosed with a rare disease at age thirty-one, comes with preconceived notions.

Many of us experience certain types of pre-judgments at one time or another in our lives. There were times in my own life when I fought hard to dissolve judgments made upon me, only to wind up back at square one with another label placed on my life. What's worse is if you allow those labels to infect your inner being.

At times, my past of being molested as a child for nearly ten years, and then being physically, emotionally, and verbally abused in a previous relationship as an adult, consumed me. I continued to fall into the role of *victim*, because I believed in and trusted the individuals who abused me.

I had to come to the realization that taking responsibility for the abuse I experienced wasn't about taking ownership for the abusers' actions. Instead, I needed to take responsibility for how I allowed those offenses to affect me. I needed to take responsibility for living the rest of my life free from the holds of being a victim so I wouldn't attract more abuse into my life.

So how could I do this? Well, for one I began looking at each abusive experience as a learning experience for myself. I decided in working to prove others wrong about the labels they placed on me. I would not let them take away my true purpose and block my growth as a human being.

I wanted to tap into the preeminent spirit within myself, not react defensively to other's opinions of me. Making peace with my past would allow me to be defined by my spirit and not my circumstances. Eliminating being labeled by negative past experiences from others and removing the damaging mental thought cycles inflicted by myself, was my goal.

I believe releasing the past is beneficial to everyone. If each of us holds the power for our own happiness, then it becomes a personal responsibility to ourselves. I found this exciting, but in the beginning it was a difficult concept to comprehend. I wanted to achieve a spiritual core with constant peace and happiness in all areas of my life. I wanted to develop a habit of viewing the waves of life with a renewed and balanced perspective.

How does one achieve and remain in that spiritual balance?

I first began with motivation to dissect the destructive inner thought processes and judgments. I allowed this habit to immerse my mind, which caused a ripple effect into my daily life and relationships. The only escape from this was to focus on the greatest of all motivations: love.

I yearned to love myself and the person I had become through those negative experiences, no matter how spiritually trying it was. I wanted to be able to share that love with others.

Have you ever heard the saying, "Hurting people hurts others"? That is what I wanted to escape. I wanted to emulate, "Loving people makes people love others." Through the practice of loving others, positive people will gravitate towards you through the overwhelming sense of your loving spirit. It warms your heart and makes you feel good, but how do you get there?

I knew my next step had to be forgiveness.

I didn't realize how difficult this would be until I turned inward to explore the hurt the labels placed on me caused. I felt that I had absolved those who had abused me, however, I had not completely forgiven.In my mind, as a protective mechanism, I held on to the pain and was not sending out true forgiveness. I needed to realize that there is only true freedom when you release the desire to change the past to 'what could've been.' The only freedom is to release it through forgiveness.

This simple action brought me peace.

In addition to forgiving those who abused and labeled me, I also needed to forgive myself. Sometimes we are very critical of ourselves, which takes us further from true peace, love, and happiness. Through a long process, I found that forgiving myself was more difficult than forgiving those who hurt me. Perhaps this is why I had a trouble-some time releasing others from the hurt they inflicted on me. I had to put my mind in a place of peace. Although they were unfortunate circumstances, could I gain something from it? Through reflection, I found lessons to enhance my character and an opening to empathize with others through their own difficulties. This created an awareness of witnessing my soul growing spiritually.

I then realized the need to absorb the knowledge of my experiences to feed my soul with inspiration for a higher spiritual level. My first lesson in manifesting came in early 2007 through a book, *Excuse Me, Your Life is Waiting* by Lynn Grabhorn and *The Secret* By Rhonda Byrne.

I began experimenting with the Law of Attraction, but would soon find myself falling back into old habits, maybe through my own fears or self-doubt. Feelings that I was not deserving of a better life were stronger than my aspirations for change. I knew this was not true and that I did deserve better, but it was hard to grasp at that time. Continuing to believe that I had no control of what life brings, I felt trapped in my past.

Despite my struggles, I knew that the Divine was trying to reach me, because in November of 2007, I was diagnosed with a rare disease called Neuromyelitis Optica, also known as Devic's Disease. I per-sonally refer to it as NMO, because it's easier to say. This disease is similar to Multiple Sclerosis, but with more frequent and severe attacks. My prognosis included a future of blindness and paralysis within a short time of five years.

The Divine and Universal laws certainly had my attention now! I knew with every fiber of my Being that in order to beat this disease, I had to keep a positive focus of loving energy. The greatest way I began moving positive energy vibrations into my body was with gratitude.

My focus changed to being grateful for everything in my life and representing that with love. This simple, but powerful practice set the tone for increasing the happiness in my life. There was not one thing that I wouldn't express my gratitude for. This led to the receiving of an incredibly powerful loving energy from everyone around me – family, friends, and even complete strangers. My beliefs changed and I realized the power of gratitude. I could literally feel the high frequency of loving energy both physically and spiritually.

In May of 2008, a medical team told me I wouldn't walk again because the damage in my spinal cord was so prominent. I didn't agree. I began visualizing myself completely healed and walking. Two weeks later I was walking. Not normally, but I was walking.

I manifested my own healing far beyond the doctors' predictions. Each day I practiced affirmations of my body healing and getting stronger. Focusing was set on my progress and not that of defeat.

In 2010, setting my intention on not succumbing to my NMO prognosis filled my inner being. I started reaching out to others with NMO in the sharing of some holistic practices that I was doing. With no surprise, the Universe responded.

A man I'll call Fred contacted me about a stem cell transplant. He was the first NMO patient to receive this. In the process, the medical team takes your own stem cells and basically reboots your immune system, similar to rebooting a computer, by reversing the damage caused by NMO. Realizing my intended goal was coming to fruition, I immediately said a prayer of gratitude and took action. I had faith that something miraculous would present itself.

In April of 2011, I underwent the stem cell transplant and my health began to turn. I'm not saying that I'm cured, because I used the process of manifestation; however, I do believe I attracted an option for me. Although not presented as a cure, the stem cell transplant puts NMO into permanent remission.

I do believe with health, and any other situation in our lives, it is powerful to use the Universal Laws of Attraction to manifest our lives into the way we want to live. I feel that in the process of any illness, medication isn't enough. You have to assist your body in the healing process by focusing on well-being, an affirmative nature, and forgiving your past hurts. When I kept to this practice, the NMO progression decreased and placed me into a perfect position to qualify for the stem cell transplant.

While I went through the intense two-month stem cell process, I read a book called, *You Can Heal Your Life* by Louise Hay. It was one of the most influential books I've ever read. It was a step-by-step guide on how to apply the Law of Attraction into your life to manifest healing. This book put me in a place of immense hope, gratitude, and love. I supported this process through inspiring music, books, conversations, and people that supported the circle of light for my future. While going through the treatments for my illness, I meditated and prayed my mantra, "Out with the bad and in with the good."

While in recovery from the stem cell procedures that included chemotherapy, I started focusing on the medical bills and the struggles that would come with it. So obviously, more bills and struggles kept coming. I recognized that I slipped from my higher plane of peace and that I needed to get back there - fast.

The next incredible book to help change my inner thought cycle was shared with me by Älska co-founder Sarah Prout, *The Game of Life and How to Play It*, by Florence Scovel Shinn. It enhanced my walk of love and gratitude. As my entire inner core turned around, so did my circumstances. It didn't erase the debt incurred from my medical treatments, but it did change my perspective.

My revived visualization now is happily paying off my debt. I focus on love and gratitude for all the bills because it came from a service that provided me with a renewal on my health. Surrounded by people with encouragement, support, and love became my life.

I revived my journey of loving others, and myself while compassionately dealing with the thoughts and feelings that weren't helping me live to my fullest potential. The Divine created each of us with a purpose, making us valuable and worthy of a fulfilled life. This cannot be accomplished without a deep understanding and acceptance of ourselves and of others. It's important to stay in your passion for life with gratitude, love, and forgiveness by expressing it and blessing others with it. This is my intention for you, to bless and inspire you through my life experience.

If I allowed the years of negative exposure to determine who I was, I wouldn't have become the champion I am today. I have no regrets or curse my past experiences, because it was all stepping stones to get me to where I am today. This gave me a greater appreciation for the beautiful people in my life and the new ones to come. I haven't got it all figured out, but I'm a lot wiser today and open to continued growth. I feel excited for the future with hope to inspire others to this deep level of consciousness. We each have the power within us to live at our highest level of well-being through love and gratitude.

No matter what past experiences or choices you have gone through, a great purpose for you is forthcoming in this life. Whether large or small situations arrive in your life, return to love. Only love can free past hurts and bring you an incredible existence. You choose the direction you want your life to go in by directing your thoughts and actions through love. Don't wait for a major life event to force a wake up call in your heart. Live in love and gratitude daily. Learn from my journey.

This is your opportunity to arise and enhance your life experience to its fullest potential. Activate the Divine within you. Each of us will face the leaving of our physical presence. In the meantime, wouldn't it be wonderful to live everyday in love enjoying all the gifts that the Universe has to offer?

Many blessings and love to you.

About the Author

Janelle McArthur is an emerging author, life coach, and an NLP master practitioner in training. She has eternal love and gratitude for her four children and soul-inspiring husband. Janelle performed vocally at countless venues around the Denver metro area with a non-profit organization to promote positive lifestyles to youth. She has a great love for singing and being creative. She has been a guest speaker at various conferences, sharing her story as an incest survivor in hopes to break the silence and bring awareness and healing.

Her spiritual faith guides her on how to love with a stronghold of hope in the utilizing of Universal laws as a reminder and guide of the inner power we all possess. She continues to be grateful everyday and would love to inspire others by sharing her life experiences. Janelle wants to create a connection with the Universal audience through understanding and oneness.

http://www.janellemcarthur.com

A PORTRAIT OF SELF-LOVE

Deborah L. Kelley

When I think of the word *self-love*, I see two boxes. One box created by unseen hands that glows with a brilliant white light and one that is steel and gray in color. Unlike the first box, the second one is self-created.

If you stand in the white box alone, you love without conditions. *No man is your enemy, no man is your friend, and every man is your teacher.* In the gray box of your own creation, you often feel victimized, unhappy, and separate from others. This one has a thick, heavy layer of guilt and fear formed by many outside influences, such as society, parents, religion, and media influences, which often set standards too high for the ordinary person.

When writing, I'm always imagining a blank canvas before me. Right now, I see a white box of light glowing inside a steel-gray cage. As a visionary artist who loves to express a dimension of life beyond the five senses, the most exciting and confusing side of me happens in the unconscious realm.

I am very sensitive to the *other side*. It has strongly influenced my entire life, and it is a great source of my creative expression. I'm always watching for synchronicities, signs, and messages to guide me down the right path of my highest good.

To get comfortable with my stories, I'd like for you to paint me in your mind as a grandmother who loves to share her dreams. I am drinking morning tea, wearing comfortable shoes, and anxious to share my wondrous vision of self-love.

This vision is actually the foundation upon which I created my novel – a personal myth – titled *The Garden of a Desert Rose*. When a friend read it, he called it *courageous writing*. I replied, "No." It is just an honest portrait of all the light and dark shades of me; however, I did not share in my novel the dream I now share with you.

At the time I wrote my novel, I was guarded about my personal faith. I wanted my novel to resonate with everyone, regardless of his or her chosen faith or belief structure. Now, I share with you... My vision of God looks like a giant tree. George Harrison of The Beatles said it best: "All religions are branches of one big tree. It doesn't matter what you call God, just as long as you call."

Our self-love canvas is awash with two boxes: one light and one dark. Now it's time to add a little color. In the center of the two overlapping boxes is a newborn baby. Her parents are watching her smile for the first time. "Oh, those are just gas bubbles," cranky, old Grandpa says, but the wisdom of light and love are locked inside this tiny bundle of flesh. She ignores Grandpa's judgment about her smile. She is too busy listening to the murmur of her mother's love and feeling the pride in her father's eyes. She has tumbled out of the all-embracing mother and father branches of love and light. Her level of consciousness, still free-floating, unattached to ego, is not fully rooted in the realm of polarity. She only knows an overwhelming desire to come learn and play on a beautiful blue-green planet called Earth.

Soon, baby grows up. She is now me of yesteryears. I'm a thirty-something, twice-divorced, single mother entering my *dark night of the soul*. I am in a state of profound grief and guilt following my second divorce. Partly looking back, it was because I was born with a passionate urge towards understanding the world in which I lived. Now, I understand nothing about myself or why I did the things I did.

How can anyone love someone they don't know? I didn't love me. Worse, I doubted my capacity to love and be loved. I was fond of my two husbands, and indeed thought I loved them. Truthfully, I did not regret either departure of marriage as much as I longed for a different past; a different story of me without all the pain, guilt, and regret. If someone had walked up to me during this period of my life and asked, "Do you love yourself?" I would've answered, "Yes." I'm the type of person who wanted to appear more normal on the outside than I felt on the inside.

My family assumed I was a little crazy because of my imaginary mind. At age five, I informed everyone I was an artist. They knew artists were often looked at as being a little crazy, so I was accepted.

I can never remember a time when I wasn't captive and driven by an inner demon. A troubling part of my psyche was compulsively hungry to create something; however, during this dark period of my life, I was passionless. I couldn't paint. I thought of Vincent Van Gogh and how his own madness destroyed his life. I feared the same was happening to me, but thankfully, I had only slipped for a while into what some call *the darkness before the dawn.*

Two days before my *dawn,* I look out my window at a hot, humid East Tennessee sky. My front yard scorched from the lack of rain. I contemplated mowing down the tall weeds before the neighbors would start complaining. I wanted no company. My level of energy was at zero. My two children were out of state visiting their father. I missed them, but was relieved I didn't have to pretend I was happy to make them feel better. My eyes began to fill with tears as I hurried out to mow the lawn.

I felt I'd stored up enough water in my tears to turn my yellow grass a deep shade of green. With each heavy step I took, I screamed upside-down prayers in my head. I told God to leave me alone and I would leave Him alone. I wanted a divorce from Him. After the grass was cut, I re-entered my house thirsty and empty of faith.

The next morning was Sunday. I don't recall why I suddenly wanted to go to church. Perhaps out of guilt or of fear that my depression was getting worse. As usual, I arrived late. I sat on the back pew and tried to make myself invisible. I am a terrible actress. I didn't want anyone to read the sadness behind my eyes, but maybe they did. After the sermon, the minister walked past me and whispered, "Welcome back." I felt an additional layer of guilt tighten around my body. After all, it was only yesterday that I asked God for a divorce.

I quickly stood up and I walked towards the bright sunlight of the open door. I hugged my small Bible and purse tightly against my chest, hoping to weave my way out of church a little faster. I almost reached the doorway when a grave faced, gray-haired lady with cold damp fingers grabbed my upper arm.

I saw her coming out of the corner of my eye. She knew my family since I was a little girl. I knew she gloried in the latest gossip, for I shamefully enjoyed hearing some of her stories. She pulled my arm so tightly that my Bible and paper bulletin scattered onto the floor. This drew more unwanted attention to me. I stooped down and spied her bent toes hanging off the end of her white old-lady sandals. I felt like throwing up. Not because of her ugly feet, but somehow, I knew she would ask me about my divorce. I was right.

"Honey," she said, the word dripping out of her mouth like snake venom. "I hear you got another divorce. You seem so pretty and sweet. What is wrong with you?"

I don't recall what I said, or how I got to my car and drove home. The person who said, "*Sticks and stones can break your bones, but words can never harm you,*" was a Buddha. That old lady's words pierced deep into my soul identity, and it hurt. I couldn't answer her question, but in her defense, she had no idea that her words catapulted me even deeper into mental anguish.

After a long fit of projecting my emotional agitation and anger of this poor women, by screaming at empty walls that didn't wear ugly old-lady sandals, I fell into a deep sleep. I found myself in a lucid state of consciousness, walking down a long dusty road. Beside me walked a man. He held my right hand in his. Energetically I knew it was Jesus. His eyes were green like the healing color of the heart chakra. He smiled down at me, and I smiled back.

He looked similar to pictures I'd seen pasted to the walls of my childhood Sunday school classroom. As we walked, a bright white light appeared in the distance. I grew excited, thinking I was getting my first glimpse of heaven. As I thought this, instantly a town appeared; however, the bright glow I'd seen from a distance was gone.

I felt horror at the gray lifeless scene that was before me. The city streets were lined with row upon endless row of prison cages stacked one atop the other. In each cage stood a person, head bent low, heavy in grief. I turned to my companion with loving gratitude for my own freedom, and asked without speaking, "Why?"

He smiled his answer back at me. "They think they need a key. Tell them, for me, the door is not locked."

Indeed, my companion was right. I looked back at the iron doors on every cage. The closed doors had a skeleton keyhole, but it was obvious to the eye the open space between the cage-like prison and the door only needed a little push to be opened.

I awoke inwardly transformed by the renewing of my mind and thankful that although I had mentally divorced God, He had not divorced me. I felt like a fireball of energy. Love feels this way. No longer did I feel ashamed of my life situation. I embraced it. For without the pain of my past, I would never have come to such a profound understanding of my psychology.

A new sense of freedom overwhelmed me. That morning, the twinkle behind my eyes had returned. I was out of my steel-gray box. Now, when the time was right, I knew someday I'd help others get out. I wanted to see, once again, the beauty of their white light as seen in a faraway sky. I felt like a newborn baby. I smiled immensely.

In manifesting self-love, remember: no key is needed.

All you need is a little push in the right direction by your Higher Power. The first Hermitic principle states *"All is Mind"*. You and I are living in an infinite part of this Loving Tree called God.

Not long after this vision, I read a book titled *Memories, Dreams, Reflections.* In a chapter titled *Visions,* Carl G. Jung described a near-death experience. In a lucid state of consciousness, he found himself adrift in a beautiful timeless space. After a period of ecstasy, he felt pulled back to his sick bed. He could hear his doctor praying for him. He felt an extreme disappointment in returning to what he called the *box system.* It gave me a second witness to the value and truthfulness of my own box experience.

Synchronicity also helped me find a metaphysical teacher, an author, whose books helped me stay out of my steel-gray box. I strongly identified with the late Florence Scovel Shinn. She was widely known in her time as an artist, illustrator, and writer. She called her light box the *perfect square of life* and advises her readers to repeat a daily affirmation acknowledging only perfect health, wealth, love, and self-expression. This, she said, would bring perfect happiness. This is not about wishful thinking. It is an active, powerful tool that I've used for over thirty years. Jesus said, "Unless you come as a little child, you cannot enter the Kingdom of God."

I pray that I have pushed you into the right direction towards a deeper sense of self-love.

Now... smile. Who cares if grumpy old grandpa thinks it is only a gas bubble.

About the Author

Deborah's paintings, as a visionary artist, display her love of nature and always incorporate a touch of the divine feminine. Her lifetime body of work includes oils, watercolor, pen & ink, and commercial illustration.

At an early age, Deborah often experienced lucid states of dreaming, conversing with deceased loved ones and electrifying archetypal figures. Upon awakening, she often felt confused about what was real and what was unreal. From this fertile ground, her inner author awoke. Her heart's desire is to paint with words, from a Southern woman's perspective, a rich and beautiful dimension of life beyond the five senses.

http://www.deborahlkelley.com

GIVING UP JEALOUSY FOR REAL

Brad Swanson

Have you ever been so jealous it destroyed everything around you? Have you ever had that pit in your stomach so bad it made you want to cry and throw up all at the same time, yet you couldn't seem to do anything about it? Ever sat there and watch yourself fall deeper and deeper into desperation and isolation while your jealous feelings overcame you and any goodness that seemed to exist within you just fell away? And that all which was left was that incessant nagging, penetrating feeling of hopelessness and certainty that you are not worthy or good enough?

Well, I have. I want to share my experience with jealousy and how I had a miraculous and lasting healing experience that literally altered my life forever.

I love women and I had always loved older ones. I was blessed with good looks as a child and always had more than enough attention from girls. I loved my babysitter who was quite a bit older than me and I always had a deep connection with her. I have a great mother so I'm sure that had a huge affect on my love and understanding of women. I know it has.

The reason this is so important in my story is because I had to go from one extreme to the other to find redemption and healing. And when it comes to romantic relationships and love, there has been no greater challenge for me as a man. Having a lot of energy from women at an early age made me feel good. It made me feel special like I was important in some way because I was cute as they would say. It gave me some special value, I thought, and I really liked it.

I was very shy as a young boy when it came to being in the presence of women, but once I was around them, I wanted to hug them and be next to them and flirt with them as much as I could. During that time in my life, I got a lot of my self-worth from them.

When I was in 6th grade, I entered adolescence's more challenging world of dealing with girls! Somewhere in the beginning of the year, some of my friends came up to me and told me that there was this older 8th grade girl named Suzie that thought I was super cute and really liked me. I remember being so surprised and happy at the same time. It felt really good. They asked me if I wanted to meet her and I agreed.

Shortly after just walking by in the hall, and kind of making eye contact and blushing, someone asked me if I wanted to be her boyfriend.

I hesitantly said, "Sure... OK." So at that moment we became boyfriend and girlfriend; so funny when you think about it now. I mean, what were we doing at that age? I didn't even know what it really meant to be boyfriend and girlfriend, but I went with it all the same. Suzie and I were in a relationship or whatever you want to call it, for like a month or so when she finally got tired of the lack of attention.

So one day, there was this special party at the roller-skating rink for the whole school and we were all going. I remember I got there a little late as my mom dropped me off. I remember walking into the skating rink all excited to see Suzie and my friends when all of the sudden one of my best friends at the time came running up to me to tell me that Suzie had just dumped me and was now going out with this older 8th grader!

I was in shock.

I remember thinking, "This can't be true." As I walked closer to the skating rink floor there she was, coming around in slow motion holding hands with this new guy. I specifically remember that feeling as my heart dropped and the pit in my stomach just ached so deeply. I had decided in that moment that there was something wrong with me and that I was not good enough. I had no idea how deeply that incident truly affected me until almost ten years later.

I spent the next ten years of my life thinking I was not good enough and always trying to get girls to like me, especially the ones who didn't. I thought if I worked hard enough or pushed hard enough they would like me. I couldn't stand it when girls liked anyone more than they liked me. I would get insanely jealous and upset. If I ever did get a girl to fall for me I would then simply drop them because there was no more challenge and I would have to move on to the next one.

I had no idea I was even doing this until my early twenties when I finally started to look at the patterns in my life and how they seemed to be completely running me. When I was twenty-one I started a path of self-awareness that literally altered my life forever. I did a seminar that showed me that all of my thoughts about life were not necessarily true or accurate and that maybe some of the things I had previously thought were not true at all. This realization completely rocked me and I began to look at all of my fears and jealousies, especially regarding women.

As I embarked on this path of healing, I began to notice how jealous I would get at different times when it came to women and at other men who might be better than me, or so I thought. If things didn't go my way, I would always have the same exact pit in my stomach that ate at me and was saying, "See? You are not good enough! You don't deserve love!"

When I was about thirty, I was living in NYC and had moved out there to pursue my acting and modeling careers. I was still deeply struggling with my insecurities and jealousy that would come up. One night as I had gone out to a club, I was having a particularly aware and conscious experience as I was doing a lot of hard work on myself and my thoughts and I had this very similar experience that was taking place. There was this girl who I liked but she was more interested in another guy. I remember that jealous feeling beginning to overtake me once again (as it always had) and I remember starting to really look at that specific feeling as it was happening. I literally was so overcome with anger and hurt that I walked out of the club. I vividly remember walking down the street of NYC while I was talking to myself about the feeling of jealousy.

What was this feeling? Why did it hurt and annoy me so bad? How come I can't get away from it? What is it really? is what I was thinking to myself. I remember going to get on the subway and asking myself the questions: do I like *me*? Do I love myself? Am I a good person? How come I feel this way? I thought, I've probably experienced jealousy a million times in my life and not one time has it ever helped me get the girl or make the situation better!

Not once!

The experience of jealousy has been with thousands of different women and not just one. All of them. As I was having all of these thoughts, I remember starting to sit down on the subway when it suddenly hit me. I thought, "Wait a second! Do I love me? Yes I do. Am I a good person? Yes I am. Not only am I a good person, I'm an awesome person. I love myself and my life. I am super fun and cool to be with. I am good looking and have a good heart." And then I thought, "Wait a second. I'm an awesome person, who the heck wouldn't want to be with me?? Who wouldn't want to be with me as I am an amazing man?!"

And it literally all stopped as I saw jealousy pop like a water balloon. Jealousy *is* a choice! And I never have to be jealous ever again. I love me and that's real. It literally never occurred to me that it was a choice. It was always just a reaction to not feeling good enough in my life. I literally was sitting on the subway and started balling like a baby. I just sat there and cried silently to myself for a few minutes. I remembered back to Suzie and 6th grade and all of the girls I had been trying to prove myself to for all those years. It suddenly all made sense! I loved me!

I couldn't believe it. I was actually having the experience of truly and divinely loving myself in a way that I never had before. This one was so huge for me I cannot even begin to explain it. There is something about romantic relationships that really mess us up the most when it comes to whatever sex you are romantically attracted to. It seems like an insurmountable task to get a handle on and that it cannot be done.

The next moment I remember thinking, "Holy crap! Can I really give this up forever?" And then I remember vividly having a deep moment of fear come over me as I saw the possibility of this. I took a deep breath and said, "I am ready."

I then made a pact with myself that the next time jealousy came up I would not grab onto it and let it go no matter what!

Only a couple days passed as something came up that started to bring up the feeling of jealousy once again. I remember starting to have that same feeling of that pit of despair. I instantly looked at it and remembered the words I said to myself as it came up: "I was not going to let it overtake me and I am going to keep my word to myself as I promised."

I watched the feeling come over me for a split second and then I took a deep breath and allowed it to flow through me like a gust of wind, and *woosh* it was gone. It makes me cry even thinking about it now as that was the first time I had ever fully honored my word to myself! I have literally not grabbed on to jealousy for more than a few seconds ever since and that was over eight years ago! That experience totally altered my life forever!

Love is a real thing that now guides my life. Learning to love oneself especially in regards to romantic relationships is the greatest gift. True love for oneself and another is possible in this real life if you are willing to do the work.

About the Author

Brad Swanson is a Love and Communication Consultant, author, creator, and host of The Male Room TV; the show that helps women understand men and men understand themselves. He has been a regular guest expert on Dyan Cannon's (3-time Academy Award Nominee) show Get Your Luv On at CBS Studios, The Speel It Show with Executive Producer Bam Erikson, and a regular on Naked Talk Radio with Elaina McMillain in Denver, Colorado. Brad was also a featured speaker at Leaders Causing Leaders at Long Beach Convention Center alongside such amazing speakers as Human Behavior Expert Candace Silvers.

"Authentic communication makes everything possible!"

http://www.themaleroom.tv

THE MANIFESTO OF ENCOURAGEMENT

Danielle LaPorte

Right now, there are Tibetan Buddhist monks in a temple in the Himalayas endlessly reciting mantras for *the cessation of your suffering and for the flourishing of your happiness.*

Someone you haven't met yet is already dreaming of *adoring* you.

Someone is writing a book that you will read in the next two years that will *change how you look at life.*

Nuns in the Alps are in endless vigil, praying for the Holy Spirit to *alight the hearts* of all of God's children.

A farmer is looking at his organic crops and whispering, *"Nourish them."*

Someone wants to kiss you, to hold you, to make tea for you.

Someone is willing to lend you money, wants to know what your favorite food is, and treat you to a movie. Someone in your orbit has something immensely valuable to give you... for free.

Something is being *invented* this year that will change how your generation lives, communicates, heals, and passes on.

The next great song is being rehearsed.

Thousands of people are in yoga classes right now intentionally *sending light out from their heart chakras* and wrapping it around the earth.

Millions of children are assuming that everything is amazing and will always be that way.

Someone is in profound pain, and a few months from now, they'll be *thriving like never before*. They just can't see it from where they're at.

Someone who is craving to be partnered, to be acknowledged, to arrive, will get precisely what they want — and even more. And because that gift will be so fantastical in its reach and sweetness, it will quite magically alter their memory of angsty longing and render it all *so worth the wait*.

Someone has recently cracked open their joyous, genuine nature because they did the hard work of hauling years of oppression off of their psyche – *this luminous juju is floating in the ether* and is *accessible* to you.

Someone just this second wished for *world peace*, in earnest.

Someone is fighting the fight so that *you don't have to*.

Some civil servant is making sure that you get your mail and your garbage picked up; that the trains are running on time; and that you are generally safe.

Someone is dedicating their days to protecting your civil liberties and clean drinking water.

Someone is regaining their sanity. Someone is coming back from the dead. Someone is genuinely forgiving the seemingly unforgivable. Someone is curing the incurable.

You. Me. Some. One. Now.

The 'What I Trust List' – Why You Need One and How to Do it.

Before a big gig or juicy-charged op moment, I do this trust exercise. I started doing it on airplanes en route to what I thought would be my destiny (even though I don't believe in destiny). After my strategic wheels have been *torqued*, and I've imagined what the ideal outcome might *feel* like, I drill into my soul foundation, to what feels so true and solid that I just might bet my life on it. Unwavering. Multi-dimensionally verifiable. Or close as I can get to it. The point: Cool my mind and warm my heart. When that's my state of being, I can respond to pretty much anything.

Often we're so busy trying to get our endorphins fired up to *go get 'em!*, we forget that feeling comforted is a very, very powerful state of being.

Create a *What I Trust List*. Whenever you need it.

Focus on the present: The whole point of this exercise is to access the trust that *already* lives in your being.

It's *not* about generating new trust, or visualizing outcomes, or affirming your way into positive thinking. Those techniques are useful, but they can also turn into mind tricks. We're concentrating on presence here.

Sometimes, the fact of the matter is: You don't fully trust that something will work out in your favor. You have doubts, you're anxious, you have reason to be cautious – and you're going for it anyway. This is the definition of courage: *Regardless of concerns, I'm givin' 'er!*

It'll be easier to give 'er if you're anchored to what's already working in your life.

Write it out: It's important that your *What I Trust List* be written out. The movement, hand to vision, will help your psyche take in the comfort. Imagine that your mind is like a lung, inhaling and exhaling as you account for all that you know to be true.

Speak it out: If you're an audio-learner, speak it out. Leave yourself a voice-mail or a voice-memo on your mobile, or talk to yourself… kindly.

Stream your consciousness: Just let it pour out. But, again, *don't include things that you don't fully have trust in.* It's okay if your list is short. Brevity is better than bravado. It could be one word if that's what feels true. It could be six pages in your day-timer if that's real.

I trust my love for… I trust my integrity. I trust how much my mama loves me. I trust that my guides are watching out for me. I trust that she'll be there when I call. I trust that there's always another idea… I trust that I can always get a job…

Go *obvious* if you need to: Nothing is too great or too small to put your trust in. Sometimes the most basic and primal things will give you a boost, especially if you're finding it difficult to think of things that you fully trust in.

I trust my next breath will keep coming. … I trust the sun will rise tomorrow. … I trust Sparky will be wagging his tail when I walk in the door. … I trust that the snow will melt. …

Trust now. Trust in *the now*. Consciously access what you know to be positively, life-affirmingly true. And that sureness will become a bridge to what's possible.

About the Author

Danielle LaPorte is the author of the bestselling *The Fire Starter Sessions: A Soulful + Practical Guide for Creating Success on Your Own Terms.*

An inspirational speaker, former think-tank exec and business-strategist, she is the creator of the online program The Spark Kit: A Digital Experience for Entrepreneurs and co-author of Your Big Beautiful Book Plan.

http://www.daniellelaporte.com

LOVE HEALS

Belinda Baillie

With all the pain and bitterness of an abused child, pouring through her consciousness in every moment, it was no wonder she was like that the day she arrived at the farm.

She stood in my doorway on that hot August day, skinny, scowling, arms folded across her chest, refusing to meet my eye. I sighed and wondered what I'd got myself into as I picked up her light suitcase and said, "Come on, I'll show you your room."

She said nothing, never even raising her gaze as she padded, pouting behind me into the house. "Here you go," I said as I plonked her bag on the bed. "You can go wash up and meet me in the kitchen for lunch."

She turned her back on me as I eyed her once again. At almost fourteen, she was short for her age. She might have been pretty with her long dark hair, intense brown eyes, and olive skin, but the hurt that radiated from her palpably was so over-powering that it was difficult to see her clearly.

I left her to unpack and headed to the kitchen. As I put salad and cold barbecue chicken onto two plates, I thought about this child I had agreed to take into my home and business for three weeks on work experience. What on earth was I going to do with her? She clearly didn't want to be here. I shook my head. Her teachers had told me there was no hope for this one. She was so bad at school that they anticipated a life of crime, prison, and unwanted pregnancy for her. Her parents didn't want her. Her mother had left her with her father, who also didn't want her. Even her social worker had given up on her. What kind of a bleeding heart did I think I was that I could get through to her?

I slumped into a chair and rested my elbows despondently on the cheerfully bright kitchen table-cloth. I was starting to question my wisdom at taking on this kid. I shook my head again and called, with more enthusiasm than I felt, "Jackie, lunch is ready. Come and get it!"

Over the next week or so, that niggling doubt grew to full-blown frustration. On a working sheep and cattle property there is always a lot to do and sitting around idly discussing one's feelings has no place. You just get on with it, doing what needs to be done.

I was supposed to be giving Jackie an idea of what a career in agriculture might be like, but we both knew that there really wasn't any point. She was just there because she had to be and I was going through the motions because I said I would.

It was the dogs that first gave me a hint that things could be different.

While she had zero people skills, the animals loved her. On a farm, working dogs are worth their weight in gold. Loyal and extremely intelligent, they are also an excellent judge of character. And my dogs were no different. They loved Jackie. And she seemed to love them equally in return, feeling more at ease with them than with me.

I watched her through the kitchen window as I washed the dishes. The way she lit up, her face shining as she romped with them, showed me a very different person from the surly teenager she was around me. It was the same with the horses. Her eyes shone and an aura of love surrounded both her and the horse when she was grooming them, getting ready for a day's work. Where she lived in the city there weren't any animals for her to engage with.

Her life, I reflected, seemed devoid of any love at all.

I wiped my hands and sat down at the kitchen table pensively. On the one hand, I was ready to send her back and give up on her like everyone else. She was just too hard. But on the other hand, I wondered what it must be like to be her? As I pondered her short life, I felt the pain of her mother's rejection, her father's drunken rages, her teachers and supposed carers not knowing what to do with her. I felt hot tears prick my eyes. To be given up on by the very people who were meant to love and care for you – what must that feel like to a child? And I had been heading in the same direction. I hung my head in shame and decided that there must be another way.

That night, as she slept, I sat outside under the clear, starry sky and asked for inspiration. This child was a living soul; a Divine spark of creation. Who was I to decide anything about her other than that she deserved love and care?

I sat there and pondered my options. I knew how to handle frightened young animals. This little one was no different. For all her bravado, she was simply a very frightened kid inside that needed love as much as anyone else. I would look beyond the phenomenon and see the spirit inside and fan that flame.

So I stopped trying *so* hard. It wasn't realistic anyway: trying so hard to make her do or be something everyone else wanted her to do or be. I wasn't being authentic either. I was trying to be encouraging and *perky* – I don't really do perky well. So I stopped and just let myself *be* myself: a farmer.

Working with animals, I knew that if you just love them without any conditions and let them come to you, they will do so in their own time if you leave the door open. So I began doing this with Jackie. I just got about my business doing what needed to be done in the farm.

I made no demands or even any attempts at conversation. I just got on with it and took her along with me, gently ignoring her, not shutting her out, but inclusive; welcoming without words, open-hearted, loving her without conversation or conditions. As with young animals, she got curious in spite of herself and slunk a bit closer, feigning indifference but ready to bolt. I would let her come nearer and watch, pretending I didn't see her.

I remember the day it began turning around for her. I was fixing a fence in the back paddock. I left her sitting in the truck as I got on with tying mesh onto a fence I'd built the day before. After a while, she got bored destroying a matchbox she'd found in there and came to investigate. I made sure I angled my body so she could see what I was doing. She was getting more curious. The more I seemed to ignore her on the outside but welcome her with my heart, the more she relaxed. She kicked at the dirt a little way off but kept pace with me as I moved along the fence.

I worked in silence for a while.

Once I felt her curiosity begin to overcome her resistance I simply said, "Want to have a go?" She shrugged sullenly. I held out a roll of tie-wire and some pliers, and pointing to a spot further along the fence-line, I said, "Why don't you go down there and do some?"

She scowled as she snatched the things from my outstretched hand and moved off, with a final toss of her head, to have a go. I had already gauged she didn't want to be taught by traditional methods. She was the type who wants to watch how it's done then have a go privately and make the mistakes without anyone else seeing so she can fix it without getting into trouble. She did the job well enough. It wasn't rocket science.

But it was a beginning.

As the days went by, she became more engaged. She began to open up a tiny bit. Her natural way with animals was giving her confidence in herself as they responded positively to her.

It was towards the end of her stay with me; another hot day. We had a young heifer in the yards that was having trouble calving. We had to help pull the calf out as this young first-time mother wasn't able to do it on her own. The implement that we use to help manually assist cattle birth was broken so we had to do it the old-fashioned way: by hand.

Now, calves as they are being born are very slippery things, so here were Jackie and I, behind this poor bellowing cow, each with a slippery leg in our hands trying to work with the contractions of the cow. We took turns, rhythmically pulling one leg of the little calf then the other. It was coming out backwards and we knew it was alive as its tail was swishing and its little legs were kicking ferociously making our job doubly difficult.

Side by side in the dust and heat, and with bushflies swarming, we worked. Shoulder to shoulder, each intended on a common purpose: to bring a calf alive into the world.

We battled in silence and finally got the calf out on the ground. But we were too late. It had suffocated in its fight to be born. We stood there dismayed and exhausted. I saw the look on Jackie's face and my heart broke. All her hopes and dreams were pinned on this little calf and we had failed it. She had come so far, but this blow may undo all the good we had done together.

I wasn't about to be defeated. I gritted my teeth and dropped to my knees there in the dust. I pounded on that little animal's chest. I lifted its slimy muzzle to my lips, covered its gooey nostrils, and blew for all I was worth to get some air in its lungs before pounding its chest again. I repeated this over and over, refusing to give up.

Suddenly the calf gave a mighty cough and came to life. I sat back on my haunches, exhausted, drawing a shaky breath and wiping my face as Jackie plopped heavily onto the ground a little way off, tears pouring down her face, silent sobs wracking her thin frame. She cried like it was the first time in her life she had been able to do so. She cried all the tears she had never allowed herself, or been allowed to cry; tears for all the times people gave up on her and all the times she had given up on herself. All the pain of her life was washing away with those tears because she saw herself in this calf and someone cared enough not to give up and brought it back to life.

That day changed Jackie's life forever. She came back to me every holiday and she learned about agriculture and animals, and how to ride a motorbike and drive a truck. She also learned how to fix fences because her driving wasn't so great. But we were doing so much more than fiddling on a farm and fixing fences. We were fixing a broken heart and bringing a soul back to life.

Jackie went on to finish high school, study agriculture, and then vet nursing. She still has an amazing way with animals. She is happily married with two lovely daughters of her own now.

But it wasn't only Jackie that was changed forever that day. I was too. I am forever grateful to that skinny, angry teenager who landed on my doorstep that hot Sunday in August. She taught me that it's worth fanning the spark and, even when it seems like there isn't any, love will find a way. By being who I was and no longer *trying*, love healed life.

About the Author

Belinda Baillie is a mentor, coach, trainer, writer, and speaker. She is the general manager of Insight Foundation, registered training organization and CEO of Global Coaching Academy.

With a variety of careers behind her, Belinda has melded her life's experience into her life's passion and purpose: to make a difference in the world through the courses she creates in mentoring, coaching, and leadership.

Somewhat quirky and intuitive in her approach, Belinda chooses to operate her business from a base of integrity, love and authenticity, teaching others to do the same. Her courses and workshops echo this attitude with her typical, down-to-earth practicality of living life as a human spirit.

She holds high level qualifications in management, coaching, acting, business, and agriculture, but her favorite things include being a part-time artist, writer, and motorcycle rider and a full-time inspirer, motivator, and mentor.

http://www.globalcoach.com.au

http://www.insightfoundation.edu.au

FROM MOTH TO BUTTERFLY

Mari Lyles

Duquesne, my home town, is a quiet, enclosed little city along the Monogahela River approximately twenty minutes from Pittsburgh, Pennsylvania. Growing up in the 1960's, it was a small but thriving town ruled by the United States Steel Company, a massive plant that continuously spewed emissions of soot and dirt all over the landscape. When the steel mill shut down, Duquesne, along with its neighboring steel towns, died a quick and very painful death.

Now, it's dilapidated, forlorn, and stripped naked of the spirit that once controlled several thousand industrious souls. Consequently, when I look back I see echoes of my life in the dull, gray, and hilly terrain, mirroring all that shaped me in that nasty little hamlet.

Growing up, all I ever wanted was to be pretty.

I wanted to be attractive; the cute one with dates; the funny, flirtatious one. Instead, I was the nerd, the geek, the four-eyed glasses-wearing troll. This was drummed into me in the fourth grade by my classmate Sam, who followed me home from school nearly every day for a year.

From the moment I left my friends on Second Street, Sam would walk up from behind, taunt me, and proclaim exactly how ugly and disgusting I was in great, outlandish detail. He would usually begin with my hair which, if truth be told, was quite pretty. However, in Sam's tongue, it was too long, too thick, and too frizzy. Whatever word he could come up with, he hurled at me.

His words would then work their way over the rest of my body.

Eyes: Too squinty and slanted.

Cheeks and stomach: Too fat.

Legs: Too skinny and knock-kneed.

Feet: Way, *way* too big.

He always saved the best for last...

His all-time favorite – his *pièce de resistance*: "You look like Porky Pig. *Oink. Oink.*"

I could have melted into the ground. I had my mom's nose – the one feature on her I detested – and I was teased about it mercilessly.

I hated Sam. Tremendously. But more so, I hated myself (my nose, my body, and nearly everything about me). I didn't realize it then, but I'd given someone else permission to define who I was.

I would love to say it only took a few months or years to empty Sam's cruel, derogatory words out of my psyche, but I'd be lying. Why? Because for the next forty years, I worried about my looks, with my hair and feet being the exceptions. And the fact that I was never quite pretty, or not pretty enough in my eyes at least, to deserve someone great. I had reached a point where I couldn't even have imagined myself ever being accepted. I had taken someone else's opinion of me and clothed myself in their negativity. Unconsciously, I'd set out to sabotage myself, making certain that I manifested just what I'd declared: unhappiness, loneliness, and rejection.

One sure-fire way I'd managed to fulfill my self-image (an unattractive troll) was eating myself to an unhealthy weight gain, and looking like a puffer fish. I'd taken on a huge layer of fat to protect myself from the outside world and I'd set up a strong guard over my emotions. I wouldn't allow anyone to creep into my world and my head, and I wouldn't accept people hurting me again if I could. I made myself that promise, and I kept that promise to my own detriment.

Looking from the outside, I had a seemingly normal and purposeful life for a while. It was rather what some people would assume to be a *golden life*. I held a well-paying job and I'd gotten married, in spite of myself, to a not-so-wonderful man who cheated on me and abused drugs and alcohol: *our family secret*. The marriage had produced two children. When I had more than I could stand of my husband's lies, cheating, and substance abuse, I divorced him. Of course the divorce led to more feelings of rejection. After all, since I hadn't been able to attract someone great and the one *not-so-great* guy cheated on me, what did that say about me?

Today I know it says I neither had relationship skills nor did I know how to make the right choices. However, back then my life was screaming, "You're a loser; nobody wants you!"

I immersed myself in church and rose to a leadership position as a deacon. Most of my time was spent there in numerous ministries to prevent me from thinking about my otherwise lonely life.

There are those things, unasked for, which can weaken and debilitate you, and then there are those things, again unasked for, which can build you up and carry you along with the tide if you allow them to do so.

I was tired of kicking against the tide and nearly drowning. I was tired of fighting all the battles in my mind, my perceptions, my images, my loneliness and my fear of never being loved. I was tired of walking into a crowd and wondering if someone would notice just how unappealing I was, and comment on it. I was tired of thinking I was crazy.

I was in that kind of drunken-tired that sinks into your muscles and bones and makes everything move in slow motion. Since I had thought of myself as crazy, I decided to immerse myself in reading. I read and reread the Bible: "As a man thinketh in his heart, so is he." And that helped to a degree. I read Neville Goddard, Marianne Williamson and Wayne Dyer, all of whom inspired me to simply get in touch with the *me* inside and simply *be*.

That too helped to a degree. Everything helped. But it wasn't enough.

Everything eventually always fell short. I went so far as having plastic surgery. And that too helped, only to a degree. The issue was that I had listened for so long, for so many years, to the gremlin in my head who'd waged war on me declaring over and over again that I was unattractive. Even with surgery, I still couldn't see myself as beautiful. Not even as pretty.

The second year post-surgery, I had had enough of me: that self-defeating and crippled loser that I'd allowed myself to become; that I'd literally made myself into. I had work to do. Major work. Then, it dawned on me. *Duh! That's what it is!* That if I didn't love *me*, why should anyone else? So, I began the monumental task of learning to love myself with preconceived faults and all. It was the most difficult, most wonderful decision I'd ever made. I understood I would never be Halle Berry or Beyonce.

This body, this life-time was what I had to deal with so my best bet was working with what I had. And I decided to work on it.

I set out on a mission to manifest a new woman, beautiful in all my glory and beautiful in all my flaws. I wrote captivating love poems to myself describing how extraordinarily wonderful I was, how wickedly funny I could be, how amazingly soft the inside hollow of my arms were, and how incredibly beautiful my lips were.

I was on a mission.

I went over every inch of my body, like God did with the formation of the earth, and declared it was good. I lost seventy-five pounds because I didn't need fat to protect my inner spirit anymore. And for the first time in my life, my words had all the power necessary to transform me. Yes, I didn't have Hollywood or classic beauty, but I had a totally unique one. When I smiled, Angels bowed down low and sang Hallelujah! Cherubim and Seraphim clapped and danced!

My beauty is breath-taking.

I shared my story with woman after woman at church in the numerous women's programs I was involved in. Here I was, helping wounded women when I had once been so wounded myself I could barely see straight some days. One of the reasons I became a coach was to pay it forward. Amazing how the Universe works.

I met so many women. Some were extraordinarily beautiful yet hated themselves and what they felt the world had done to them. There were women whose self-talk had been as lethal as mine. Women who had adopted someone else's definition of who they were. Women whose bodies had been raped and minds had been twisted by relatives and family friends. Women who'd contemplated suicide and murder. Women who'd wanted to love but felt themselves unworthy or too damaged to love.

All I had to offer them was what I'd learned on my journey: *it all begins from within.*

These are the things I shared with them, and I'm now sharing with you.

Celebrate *You*!

Make it a point to celebrate your life regardless of who joins the party. If it's just you with one glass of champagne and a bag of chips, don't let that stop you from acknowledging the fact that you're a gift from the Universe, and you deserve a celebration.

Accept Your Imperfections

You will not look perfect, act perfectly, or be perfect in this lifetime. An old saying goes that the day you become perfect, you will become a Messiah, and we all know what happens to Messiahs. Life is a journey: one full of adventures, misadventures, thrills, and some sorrows thrown in for good measure. It's our duty in the journey to take our imperfections, learn whatever lessons lie in them, and move on. Look at imperfections for what they are: guideposts along your journey.

Loving Yourself is the Most Important Choice You Will Ever Make

Every moment of every day you get a chance to determine who you will be, how you will think, and the choices you will make. Loving yourself is simply a matter of choice. You can certainly choose not to and stay miserable or you can decide that you're worth the skin you're in.

The Extent To Which You Love Yourself, is the Extent To Which the World Loves You in Return

It was amazing that shortly after I determined to love myself, the Universe did a big thumbs-up. My whole life did a 360-degree turn. I consciously decided that I was entitled to be respected and deserved all the good things I began receiving. The more I moved in my new mind-set, the more the Universe complied with my thinking. The Universe is an abundant place, and as a child of the Universe, why not share in the abundance?

You, and You Alone, Determine Your Level of Self-esteem

Every child must have heard the old saying: "Sticks and stones can break your bones, but words can never hurt you." What a crock! Words can destroy you if you let them. But whether or not you permit someone else's words to be the definitive authority in your life is a choice you make. Shut down others' chatter and consciously choose whose words you will allow to define you – those from someone else, or constructive words you speak to yourself. With every positive word you speak to yourself, your esteem goes higher and higher.

See Clearly

I know from experience that people who don't love themselves tend to fantasize and have vivid imaginations. As long as you hold on to fantasies, you will never experience the reality of your greatness. Clear your mind of insignificant clutter, others' opinions, and visualize yourself as the Universe sees you: full of wonder and beauty.

It's only then that you'll be set on a path of discovering your true self-worth.

About the Author

Mari Lyles is a certified life and relationship coach, having graduated from iPEC (Institute for Professional Excellence in Coaching) and RCI (Relationship Coaching Institute). Her background of over twelve years as a mentor and counselor, and now coach to abused and molested women and her *cheerleading* mindset, led to her decision to attend iPEC, one of the nation's premier life-coaching schools. There, she completed the courses as a certified professional coach and energy leadership index-master practitioner. Upon certification, she began coaching women on life-changing relationships. Not satisfied with two certifications, Mari enrolled in the Relationship Coaching Institute, the country's oldest and most distinguished relationship coaching school, to define and hone her craft.

Mari is an expert writer for task.fm.com, and comments on relationships, spirituality, and abundance. Her articles have also appeared in pathjoy.com and examiner.com.

http://www.mybeautifulrelationship.com

THANK GOD I DIDN'T KILL MYSELF

Jenny Parker

You don't come out of a womb at ten pounds having devoured everything in sight for nine months and leaving your mother a wreck of skin and bones without a reason. Looking back, I was hungry my entire childhood: hungry for love that would fill the emptiness I felt inside. Being born into a pretty normal Australian family, it was a little hard to understand.

In my childhood years, I continued to find temporary relief by numbing my pain with food; trying to build layers of protection from life with my own flesh. I stole food, stole money to buy food, and cooked food at every opportunity. Most of what I ate passed straight through without giving any nourishment at all. The emptiness of life continued well into adulthood. Even after filling the void enough to lead a functional life, I still felt emotional pain and didn't know what it would be like not to feel this pain or emptiness.

Mum and Dad officially separated when I was fifteen, although unofficially it happened years prior. It catalyzed the beginning of a twenty-year alcohol addiction for Mum that would see her in just about every mental institution and detox-clinic in Sydney. With Mum fighting for her life and Dad building his business empire 1,700 kilometers away, parental guidance was scarce. My coping mechanism was to adopt the rebel archetype and run amok. I hit cigarettes, drugs and alcohol as hard as I could. I had found more powerful ways to drown out my feelings. The only reason I didn't kill myself was because my body couldn't take the hard stuff. There, but for the grace of God, I went.

By the age of seventeen and still at school, my weekend job as a cashier at the local chicken shop didn't cover the costs of my consumptive lifestyle. I started selling drugs to keep up my addiction and was stoned every day.

My short-lived life at twenty-one had beaten me down so much that I decided I wasn't much good to anyone or anything. I was finding it increasingly difficult to function and connect with people and thought I was going mad. I didn't want to live out my life as a mad person so made the decision to end it all. In a strange way the decision was a relief. But I was a mess: I could barely boil water for a cup of tea, let alone embark on a suicide mission. My wrist-slitting project only produced cuts that required a trip to the nearest hospital for stitches.

Not long after, I was contemplating jumping from tall buildings preparing for another exit strategy, when my step-mother lifted my spirits by telling me I wasn't going mad but that I had suffered a nervous breakdown and that I could recover from this condition.

It was my first glimmer of hope.

She convinced Dad to let her take me to a palm-reader; a far more attractive idea than Dad's suggestion of a psychiatrist. The palm-reader said, "You have a very long life ahead and the potential to heal and to be happy". I burst into tears.

I didn't know whether it was because I felt hopeful for the first time ever or because I felt despaired at the prospect of having to get on with it. At that moment, I had an epiphany where I saw that wherever I went, there I would be, so I might as well sort out my mess in this life, rather than having to get a new body and start again. Within my wounded heart I then knew I had what it took to live a life of joy; I just had to find the way forward.

This awakening didn't key out the unconscious self-destructive patterning that lay beneath the surface. It led me to look for joy in all the wrong places. I chose a life style that wrote out a death warrant, living life on autopilot through sex and drugs and rock and roll. By then, I was completely numb to how I was feeling.

I continued to sell drugs to supplement my habit, drove my car, motor-bike, and bicycle like a maniac, and generally lived dangerously wherever I could. I was a runaway train; operating from survival mode and programmed for demolition.

People find all sorts of ways to imprison themselves. Some do it with an addiction or relationship; some with a mental or physical illness; while others have a fear of the unknown and will never venture out into that realm. And some of us create a situation that literally puts us behind bars. The latter strategy ended up being the one that saved my life. I was arrested for selling cocaine to the general public.

When they photographed, fingerprinted, stripped and hosed me down, I felt that I couldn't possibly stoop any lower. The sound of the officer locking me in my cell was a stone-cold and deeply sobering experience.

It was two days before I drummed up the courage to phone home and tell my family.

I was dreading the call and was more concerned about letting them down than myself. Dad went grey overnight. It was a double-whammy because my lovely brother was just about to spend a year in prison for similar offences. Mum was devastated. She felt someone should be with me, but knew that she wasn't strong enough to face the mission. My gorgeous sister volunteered and jumped on a plane to be with me for a couple of weeks.

When I was sentenced, the judge said, "You are obviously an intelligent person from a good family and should know better." And with that, he handed me a three-year sentence that reflected this. Being locked in a cell slowed me down enough so that I could view the movie of my whole life without distraction. It was an excruciatingly painful and ugly sight. What had I achieved? What sort of person was I? I couldn't access any hope for the future. I was drowning in my self-loathing and was terrified about what I would do when I came out of prison. In my heart I knew that I couldn't continue with past activities but I was addicted to the money, and I wasn't qualified at anything that would keep me in the lifestyle to which I had become accustomed.

Forced to face myself and unable to numb my feelings with alcohol and drugs, the journey became horrendously intense. I got to a point where I didn't think I could take it any more. Yet I did.

The backlog of feelings that came up was overwhelming. I reached a pivotal point where I realized that I wasn't going to survive unless I stopped judging myself and just accepted myself as I was: warts and all. This was a breakthrough. I had inadvertently started my healing journey. As Churchill once said, "If you are going through Hell, keep going." And that's exactly what I chose to do.

When I had sciatica for a few months I put it down to sitting on hard wooden prison chairs for so many hours in the day. Around the same time a friend sent me the Louise Hay book *You Can Heal Your Life* which talks about the psychological sources of pain. When I found out that sciatica was linked to a fear of the future, security, and finances, I decided to stop worrying about them.

The pain disappeared overnight and never came back.

Such is the set-up of the prison system that only one out of three prisoners doesn't reoffend. I was fortunate to break free. At the beginning of my sentence, an officer said to me, "Make the system work for you." This struck a chord and I came out nineteen months later to a new home and a new job in a trendy design company. I had transcended my drug addiction and was able to start a new life with new friends.

Apart from my sister, I hadn't seen my family for five years by the time I returned home for a holiday. When I saw my dear wise Dad, he was blown away by how different I was. With Aussie humor at its best, his first comment was, "If I had have known how well you would turn out I would have put you in there myself!"

After two years I took over the design business and became very successful within the heart of London, rubbing shoulders with the creative, rich, and famous. I was living the high life of monetary success. I had almost everything I had ever dreamt of having, but after seven years it still wasn't enough to make my heart sing. Somewhere inside, there was still a deep empty abyss.

I had learnt from my past mistakes, so instead of fighting my destiny, this time I surrendered, and allowed the Universe to suck me into place. I acted on the whispers I heard and proactively took steps to change instead of waiting until the Mack truck ran me over.

Following my heart's knowingness, I sold up, returned home and moved back in with Mum for a while which enabled us to heal and transform our war-torn relationship into harmony and into a deep love and respect for one other. I discovered that it's never too late to have a happy childhood. Mum too has turned her life around and is a powerful inspiration for myself and anyone who gets to meet her or hear of her journey.

I embarked on a career in healing; working with body, mind, and spirit. After forty years of resisting my puzzle piece I finally tapped into the purpose for me being here. In the beginning it was focused on fulfilling my personal life task to heal my own wounding. As I healed myself, my remedy started to naturally expand out to helping others too. These days I'm also teaching and writing. When we are doing what we came to do, no matter what it is, life flows. It never feels like I'm going to work, I just get to do what I love every day. My heart sings. It's the most incredibly warm feeling of wholeness and love that the world can neither give nor take away.

Although I would most definitely not recommend the path I walked and if I had my time again I would do it very differently, there is no use lamenting over wasted years; no use to cry over spilt milk. I learnt to stop looking back with regret, or ahead with fear, and started to look around with awareness, where I can turn the drawbacks into blessings. I feel like I have fallen into just about every pitfall that can present on the path and then found a way out and it now brings me the greatest privilege and pleasure to assist others to experience a more graceful journey.

It doesn't matter what happened in the past; what matters is how you feel about it now.

The key for me has been to stop avoiding, resisting, and rebelling against feelings. I simply need to acknowledge and accept them as they are without judgment. Feel how I feel and be grateful for absolutely everything. This is the alchemical key that allowed all my fears to be transformed into love and beyond. I learnt that I have a choice between love and fear in each and every moment. And guess what? I choose love.

Feelings are the eyes of the heart. I have chosen the path of the heart master and wish only to leave a trail of love in my footsteps. I would like to express my appreciation to you, the reader, for allowing me to share my story with you. Wishing you a life that is full and overflowing with love and joy if that is your desire. From my experience it doesn't get much better than that.

About the Author

Jenny Parker is a woman of the world. She has had many adventures in her quest to find the beauty of self, including riding across the Nullarbor on a bike (the stark, treeless plain between Perth and Adelaide in Australia) and sailing half-way around the world on a yacht. She has had many careers, including a design business in London, England.

For the past eleven years Jenny has been officially working as a healer, writer, ascension mentor, teacher, and inspirational speaker. Jenny's vision is the transformation of humanity to compassion and joy, and the restoration of planetary health. She shares that, "My mission is to fully embody heart mastery and wisdom on all levels of my being, and to inspire others to do the same."

In her own playful way, she creates laughter and a brighter outlook wherever she goes.

http://www.heartforce.com.au

THE GEOMETRY OF LOVE

Adele Ryan McDowell

Like a fish swimming towards the surface, I move out of a deep sleep and into the complete darkness of a strange place. Where am I?

I bolt upright in bed and blink madly. *What is that?* There, circling around the room, at a fairly decent clip, is a large, bright-green geometric figure; some kind of quadrilateral. This is a first: a flying symbol.

I switch on a light and my green friend disappears. *Was that real? Or was it my overactive imagination?* I take in the room and regain my bearings. I am in a bed-and-breakfast in the UK, presenting at a conference for burned-out healthcare professionals. I look at the clock and discover that I have been asleep for only a few hours.

I jump out of bed and, for some unknown reason, grab the conference brochure. There is a workshop on a new healing methodology by a Michael Dunn; an entry I have never noticed before. I mark the page, go back to bed, and sleep well. So well, in fact, I remember little of my middle-of-the-night awakening until two days later.

In the morning, I head to Michael's workshop and take a seat in the front row. Michael is tall with graying hair, blue eyes, and an intelligent face. He starts out nervously, utters a swear word, and is mortified. "Oh, this is going to be fun," I think. I am going to enjoy this very human guy. Michael inspires us with his new way of thinking and different approaches. Everyone wants to talk to him, including myself. I have a thousand questions on how can I use his work to help my clients.

Alas, Michael is surrounded by so many people that I opt to meet my friends for lunch in the refectory of the retreat house. When Michael later sits at the far end of our table, I applaud his workshop and he bows in acknowledgment.

Outside, after lunch, our paths intersect again. This leads to an unexpected, playful afternoon with a long walk through the countryside and non-stop conversation over tea. There is something magnetic and all-too-familiar going on between us. We have difficulty parting; we maintain eye contact as we each walk in opposite directions.

We agree to meet again, several days later, in a London park. The day is movie-perfect. We stroll along the pathways until we come upon umbrella-striped lawn chairs. As we lower ourselves into the close-to-the-ground chairs, we dive into the deeper waters of connection. The world seems to stop as we unveil layer upon layer of our individual stories. I am surprised at how easily we reveal ourselves to one another. There is no hesitancy or obfuscation and the conversation is free flowing. We share the good, the bad, and the ugly as if we have known each other forever.

This deeply intimate conversation heightens the palpable chemistry between us. We acknowledge the heat, but given Michael's girlfriend, we choose not to act. I walk Michael to the tube station and we hug good-bye.

I head home to the United States and discover I am a changed woman. Let me explain: Within 24 hours of leaving London, there are three, highly unusual events that happen in my life. I attribute these surreal happenings to the shift in my energies given my time and connection with Michael.

- A younger gentleman, sitting next to me on the plane, spends the entire seven-hour transatlantic flight trying to convince me to have an affair with him.

- As I leave for work the next morning, the apartment superintendent straddles the hood of my compact car with his arms folded against his chest. He demands to know where I am going.

- As I exit the parking lot of my apartment complex, an unknown gardener unexpectedly turns his body, faces me, and repeatedly blows kisses at me.

Really? I feel like I am visiting an alternative Universe. These kinds of things never happen to me. As Mother Marcella told me in sixth grade, "Adele, you are an excellent second banana." I am the type of woman who is the sidekick, the Ethel Mertz to your Lucy Ricardo. I am the person the guys came to for advice, not usually the focus of their attention.

Once I get home, I begin to connect the dots. Prior to the conference, my intuition told me that I was going to meet someone who would become important in my life. I can now name that person in three syllables. Hilariously – and not-so-ironically – the workshop I presented at the conference was entitled *Symbolism: A Portal of Consciousness*. That certainly explains the flying green geometry. And one of my workshop participants, to say thank you, had given me a huge chocolate egg wrapped in gold. More symbolism.

My intuition's whisper, the workshop on symbolism, the circling green geometry, and the golden egg are clear signs the gods are talking to me. It, however, takes me a long time before I fully understand the message.

Over the next few years, Michael and I share intermittent emails and a tender visit at London's Heathrow airport. I ask Michael if he is open to me talking to him in the ethers. He says sure, but I sense a raised-eyebrow with his acquiescence. Funny thing is, Michael answers my etheric questions in his emails, and later, in person.

Time and distance do their things. Our lives take separate turns and our communication and contact became rare.

Four years later, I plan a protracted trip to England. I love it there and have visited frequently over the years. The United Kingdom feels like my spiritual home. I nudge a friend to help me find a place to stay; this time, for some inexplicable reason, I have a need to be in the London area.

Days before I am to leave the United States, Michael emails. This is totally out of the blue; he asks if I am coming to the UK soon. "Yes, as a matter of fact, I am," I say. He offers to pick me up at the airport and take me to the home of my hostess. I say, "Yes!" with a huge grin on my face.

It has been a very long time.

Reconnecting in London, we metaphorically bump heads and find ourselves out of sync like two discombobulated teenagers. Michael is at a juncture in his life where he is questioning everything. He feels stuck and is facing the fork in the road; whereas, I have just taken a leap of faith with my professional life and am free-falling into the unknown.

There is, also, an acknowledged, but unspoken, sexual tension that is driving us both to distraction. We know that once the spark is ignited, we will become highly combustible. So, we circle one another like cats: focused, hyper-vigilant, utterly still, and waiting for one of us to pounce.

Before I arrive in London, Michael has dreamt that he is going to die soon. This is particularly disturbing as Michael has a long history of prescient dreams. He is rattled and apprehensive. His coloring is off and his vitality diminished. Michael allows me to do some hands-on energy work. When he returns to the living room after the healing, he grabs me in an embrace.

And so it begins. On a summer afternoon, a wonderfully passionate, heart-opening, energy-shaking love affair.

We fall into each other's company easily. We walk London in the afternoons; on weekends, we take drives into the country. Michael sings me love songs as we bask in London's night glow. We stroll, hand in hand, through a small village and watch the Thames curl under the moon. We sip tea and talk psychology. Michael grounds my energy; I massage his shoulders and work out the kink in his back.

And when we are alone, we energetically move each other to different realms and to old memories with blinking visions of Egypt, Newgrange, and a coastline far away.

Through the communion of our energies, we heal each other. We open the floodgates of the divine masculine and feminine. We wake each other up; we remember who we are and who we were. We refill the empty chalice in one another and, in the process, we both become revivified.

And beyond the transcendent aspects, this is also a real-world relationship. It is full of the push-and-pull of pain and pleasure, disappointment and delight, fury and acceptance. Michael's life is complicated; there are no easy choices. It is painful. We know what we must do: end our relationship. And, in the long run... this is exactly how this is meant to be.

At the end of our summer, Michael chooses the familiar path and I take the road not taken. We both are heartbroken and suckerpunched with grief. It is very tough going for awhile. We do not want to break apart, but there are worldly considerations and we know, from a higher perspective, that it is the right decision. It takes some time, but, eventually, we find our way out of the heartache.

From Source, there comes a drop of light, of yin and yang, which becomes two identical souls, magnetically resonant, who go forth with an identical blueprint to grow and learn. Each soul manifests its blueprint differently. Throughout lifetimes, these souls, known as twin flames, come together to teach, help, and catalyze one another in soul growth and development. They share a deep and profound love that is not always explainable. There is a continuous, magnetic connection. One twin flame's soul growth aids the other; they are inextricably bound souls of light.

Michael and I come to understand that we are twin flames and, as such, our relationship is destined to end. Twin flames are not meant to be together on a permanent basis in the human earth-plane sense; this hinders the respective soul trajectory and growth. Yet, twin flames never say goodbye; they always stay connected on an eternal soul level.

Needless to say, this is very challenging on the human level, but *Twin Flame School* gave Michael and me the opportunity to learn to love from a higher perspective and this, after all, is the primary objective and ultimate purpose. We were given the greatest gift and the hardest lesson: to learn to love unconditionally.

These days, Michael and I operate from a higher perspective with one another. We allow the light to flow between us and give each other the space for our souls to flicker and shine in their own unique way.

Remember that circling green quadrilateral? I later identified the quadrilateral as a parallelogram and this makes twin flame sense to me: Michael and I are connected as one unit on a parallel path. And, green, of course, is the color of the heart.

And remember the gift of the golden egg? The egg represented the new life, which we certainly found with one another. The gold color embodied the glow of Source and it was that high-octane vibration that allowed us to shift into a higher perspective.

The gods certainly spoke to me. It took time and many heart-opening experiences for me to learn the geometry of twin flame love: parallel paths, equally connected, always in movement, and forever in love and light.

About the Author

Adele Ryan McDowell, PhD., is a psychologist, teacher, and writer who came to her current place in life through the frequent and not-so-subtle prodding of the gods. She likes looking at life through the big viewfinder and is a perpetual student who believes in the power of an open heart and a good laugh.

Adele is the author *Balancing Act: Reflections, Meditations, and Coping Strategies for Today's Fast-Paced Whirl* and *Making Peace with Suicide*. She is a contributing author to the Shift Awareness anthologies: *2012: Creating Your Own Shift* and *The Sacred Shift: Co-Creating Your Future in a New Renaissance*. Adele's next book is entitled *Help, It's Dark in Here*.

Adele – a Texan by birth – is an upbringing, and pioneering spirit who lives in Connecticut in the United States where you will find her driving along the highways and byways, singing loudly in her car.

You can learn more about Adele and her writing from her website.

http://www.adeleryanmcdowell.com

IT'S ALL ABOUT HOW YOU FEEL BECAUSE FEELINGS ARE MAGNETIC

Vienda Maria

I first discovered the power of thoughts and manifesting when I was in my late teens. I would notice the discrepancy between how some of my friends and I were served in our favorite café. Those who were living their lives with high anxiety and a general distrust of others and of life, would often have unfortunate results: their coffee would be spilt; their order would come out late; the waiter would be abrupt or unfriendly. Those of us who had positive thoughts and expectations about life would have the exact opposite. We would get discounts, free food, and a lovely service.

This is in exactly the same café, often at the same time.

I then discovered that when I changed the way I thought and felt about myself, I could change the way life proceeded and how I experienced it.

Putting this discovery into practice is akin to being an alchemist, turning everyday life participation into a magical adventure where anything is possible. We all have the capacity to do this.

Unlike other creatures, human beings have been given an indefinite nature and thereby the ability to mould and change both ourselves and our experiences. We have the choice to change how we think, concurrently changing the way we feel and experience anything.

This is manifesting.

By its substance, manifesting implores you to investigate the relationship you have with yourself above all else. This is because manifesting is a reflection of who you are, the thoughts you have, and the things you say and do.

The Secret of Manifesting

The secret of manifesting is living from your heart.

This means coming from a place of authenticity, self-acceptance, and self-love. It is a feeling practice. After all, feelings *are* magnetic. And you cannot feel with your head. You feel with your heart. And to be able to feel with your heart you have to get honest with yourself; really honest.

To clear the pathway of manifesting, you must fully accept yourself, just as you show up in every moment.

Because it demands self-awareness, self-acceptance is the cornerstone to allowing the magic of creating your world with your thoughts. The clearer you are with your authentic self, the more speedily and direct the pathways to manifesting become. Behind authenticity lurk the fundamental values and beliefs that you have garnered over time in relation to how you have been socialized (taught to behave in a certain way and conform to society).

Following social norms however is not necessarily authentic. In fact this is rarely the case.

Being authentic means being a warrior on your own course, viewing life as an adventure, experimenting with what works for you, and letting go of what doesn't. Letting go of expectations, results, and trusting that the Universe will conspire to present you with an unrivalled outcome, even when it appears in a form unlike anything you could imagine, makes life gentler, smoother, and better.

Self-acceptance, and thereby letting go of control, is a choice that you get to make every moment of each day.

How to Live from the Heart

When you live from your heart (the source of your feelings and emotions) and make peace with yourself, you learn to love and accept yourself fully. From this place you can easily and quickly conjure up anything in your life that is in alignment with your authentic self. Self-acceptance is a mental note and sensation that you are worthy of all the good you experience and imagine. It is a practice until it becomes an innate habit.

- Decide now that, no matter what, you fully accept yourself.

- Give yourself a break and don't be so hard on yourself. You are wonderful and deserving.

- Use affirmations like the one made famous by Louise Hay: "I love and approve of myself." She recommends saying this at least a hundred times a day.

- Become attentive to your thought patterns and to when you subject yourself to negative self talk. Self-depreciating thoughts result in feeling bad about yourself. In fact, a recent study, according to *My Health News Daily* website, shows that when we engage in negative self talk we may feel the effects for several weeks afterwards as well as increase the risk of depression.

- Give up on guilt and on feeling badly about yourself. A positive self image is essential and can be easily cultivated. Focus and build on your strengths. Celebrate your achievements and generously accept praise and compliments.

Self-acceptance is enigmatically linked to self worth and confidence. Simply by believing in your own skills, talents, unique eccentricities, and whole being, fully brings you in line with who you are and gives you a precise sense of clarity. This clarity makes manifestation powerful. When the thoughts, fears, and expectations of oneself are resolved, a clear path is created for one's thoughts to become real. You are no longer caught between the physical nature of your being and the spiritual expression of yourself. These two parts experienced as duality become one whole.

There is No Right or Wrong

It's all about perspective. You judge events and experiences to be either good or bad. But in fact, events are neither nor. They are simply what they are: contrasts of experience. There is no objective truth.

Choose to be positive by taking your current situation into perspective.

Many years ago, a friend of mine taught me a great trick. In any less-than-lovely situation she would say, "Well, what is the worst thing that could happen?"

This puts anything into perspective because you realize that you're allowing your mind to grasp hold of your imagination and go on a thrilling theme park ride through the worst possible scenarios. It places a light on what you're experiencing, brings you back to awareness, and adds a little humor when you realize just how silly your worst fears are and how unlikely they are to come true.

Even if the worst possible case scenario does happen, you have the facility to deal with it. It's how you respond to and feel about the experience that transforms it.

Surrendering to Life Experience

Feeling how you feel is infinitely paramount in the art of manifesting. This is illustrated easily by the days when we feel good about ourselves and the world, is just peachy. Everything goes right in comparison to the days in which a dark grey cloud seems to be hovering over our esteemed heads when we might as well have stayed in bed.

Our external, physical life experiences are reflected by our inner perceptions.

It's on the days that things aren't going so well, that we have the most opportunity to grow and refine our lives and how we feel. One of my own habits in the past has been to push and fight against what was occurring. If I thought a situation wasn't in line with where I saw myself, I refused surrendering to it and refused accepting the situation for what it was. Struggling against what something *is* and what *is not*, is what causes the pain that we experience.

Often, it appears that there is nothing more challenging than practicing the art of self-acceptance when things are tough. You're unwell, stressed out, overwhelmed, tired, and have allowed daily life to get the better of you. This moment of frustration however, is a glorious key to unlocking your potential. It's not the situation that causes us woe; it's how we choose to respond to it that does. This moment gives you the opportunity to become aware of what has surfaced for you. Don't feel bitter about it. Choose to let go and change your way of thinking around it. This will pave the way for you to heal.

Your Inner Compass

We have been taught to bulldoze our feelings as if they don't matter and just to keep doing what we are doing; following our schedules and the demands of others. And yet, we still expect our lives to change.

Your feelings are incredibly valuable as they act as a compass showing you the direction you are facing. Our modern lifestyles leave little room for the sensitivity required to really feel and act accordingly. Take time out for yourself. Give yourself the space to *just be*. Consider how you are living life: is it in line with your *own* beliefs and values? If not, adjust and tune it accordingly. Make life simple.

Result: Enjoy and savor your life all the more.

Self-acceptance often means taking the road less travelled as for once you are listening to your own inner thoughts; conjuring and doing what is uniquely right for you. Not for anyone else: For you. Because this is your life. For your life to show up as you wish and to be distinctively yours, you only have to get clear on who you are and fully accept yourself.

Know Your True Nature

Clarity and razor-sharp focus within yourself and how you feel, knowing your true nature, brings you closer to what you really want. Generally speaking, you are yearning for a sense of wholeness, security, and belonging. You want to feel good. Always look within yourself first. Without the answers you seek, you shall not find.

I find that on a daily basis, the more I accept myself, the better, smoother, and happier life is. Of course I still experience the highs and lows that provide the contrasts of human experience, but self-acceptance allows me to remain centered and present with all that is. It fully embraces and nurtures all that you are; the exact way you show up in each and every moment.

Whether you show up in a good mood or not, it gives you the presence for self awareness and the ability to change how you are feeling without judgement. It brings awareness into the moment. It allows you to feel where you're at and let go of habitual thoughts and behaviors that are no longer supportive. Self-acceptance encompasses many variables including integrity, authenticity, knowing oneself, and an inherent sense of self-worth and confidence. Finding that centered space in your heart where you fully accept yourself is your sweet spot and where all the magic happens.

You are a physical manifestation of love, experiencing the unfolding of life with all its choices, contrasts, and human virtues. You are the center of your life experience.

And from that center you have the ability to create *anything* you want.

About the Author

Vienda Maria is a life coach, philosopher, and wordsmith who waxes lyrical on self love and consciousness. She lights up when she shares the message of living life on your own terms – after all, it's all about truth, love, and self-realization.

http://www.viendamaria.com

HOW TO FEEL BLISSFULLY COMFORTABLE IN YOUR OWN SKIN

Lisa McCourt

Sounds nice, right? So what's keeping you from it and why don't you just claim it? The only thing standing between you and that kind of freedom and confidence is your inability to live authentically from your innermost core. Notice that I'm not telling you to be authentic because it will make you a better person, or because you owe it to the world or anything like that. I'm telling you to be more authentic because authenticity and self-love are your keys to the kingdom. Without them, nothing else can bring you joy. With them, nothing can fail to bring you joy.

We all started out gloriously authentic, but our authenticity was beaten out of us. Over and over, we got the message, implicitly and explicitly, that, "Image is everything," and, "You don't get a second chance to make a first impression." My friend who works in sales for a mega-publishing company likes to quip, "Anybody who says you can't judge a book by its cover never tried to sell one." The cover is all we judge by!

And all of us want our covers to be the shiniest, most impressive covers we can manage to project. But where does that really leave us in terms of self-love and genuine connection with our fellow humans? Our inauthentic tendencies are often woven so deeply into the fiber of our beings that we have no idea they're even there. People-pleasing is an all-too-common and insidious addiction in our world, and I know I will forever be a recovering addict in that regard.

At the root of all people-pleasing tendencies, and most inauthentic tendencies in general, is a fear of being judged. Many of us grew up with some degree of a fear of abandonment from being found unlovable if we were judged and came up short. And we all judge ourselves to varying extents. If you think you don't judge yourself, it probably just means you have a judgment about judging yourself.

If you're sensitive to the criticism of others, consider this: The extent to which you feel hurt by anyone's judgment of you is directly proportional to the degree to which you subconsciously judge that trait in yourself. If I called you a jerk, you might feel insulted, because most of us have a fear, deep down, that we have the capacity to be jerks. But if I called you a rhinoceros you'd probably just think I was nuts and shrug it off. You know you're not a rhinoceros, so there's no way I can insult you with that – unless you have a big nose or a big butt that you're sensitive about, in which case your own self-judgment would cause you to be insulted.

When you catch yourself in those inevitable moments where you're not expressing your deepest truth, celebrate it! Celebrate it because you caught yourself and that means – in that moment at least – you're glimpsing your real self. Any acts of self-improvement must always start with awareness. Becoming ever more aware of the masks you wear will have the marvelous effect of revealing to you – by way of contrast – the one who resides beneath those masks. That's who you're looking for. That's who you want to love.

Steps to Start You Living More Authentically Today:

1. Every time you catch yourself saying yes when you want to say no, smiling when you feel like scowling, or nodding politely through a long conversation you'd rather walk away from, say the words, "Not me," silently in your head. You won't be able to change long-held patterns overnight, but just starting to identify them to yourself will put you on the right track.

2. Once you've begun noticing which people and situations bring out the *inauthentic you* most frequently, make a list of the perks of that relationship or situation. What are you getting out of it? You may find that you get very little from it, and choose to extricate yourself from those situations.

3. If you find that you do get substantial benefit from remaining in the situation that you've been inauthentic in, start looking for small ways to introduce more of the real you into that situation.

Sometimes an honest, heartfelt conversation is all that's needed to clear the air and get you some breathing room. Give the other person the benefit of the doubt, and go into the conversation with the full expectation that you'll be liked and respected even more for demonstrating your authenticity. ("Mom, I'm so touched by how much you love to cook for me, but tonight I really feel like something lighter. Let me take you out for sushi instead.")

Worst case, Mom will be offended, but if you consistently express your truth with love and compassion, she'll get used to the new you and it will eventually inspire her to be more of who she really is as well. Authenticity is the surest route to deepening your relationships with others as well as your relationship with you.

About the Author

Unconditional love expert Lisa McCourt is a dynamic speaker, seminar leader and author whose thirty-four books have sold more than 5.5 million copies worldwide. Her new book, *Juicy Joy – 7 Simple Steps to Your Glorious, Gutsy Self*, teaches people to embrace *radical authenticity* to fully experience unbridled joy in life. Lisa lives in South Florida with her two children. For a free Juicy Joy audio program, visit Lisa's website.

http://www.lisamccourt.com

HAPPILY EVER AFTER

Mark H. Kelly

I've heard it said before that the story of Cinderella is really an allegory for the power of intention, in that while she knelt cleaning the ashes from the fire place, she focused on the better life she wanted to create and called forth the fairy godmother within.

I don't know whether this is the case or not. But for what I'm about to share with you, it doesn't really matter, as getting the *prince* – around which most tales and teachings about manifesting revolve – is but the start of a much bigger manifestation called *and they all lived happily ever after*.

This is where all fairytales stop, yet, ironically, this is where the deeper truth about manifesting, love, and oneness starts, for it is this dream of *happily ever after* that humanity as a whole mistake for liberation from the pain and suffering of life.

In my story oneness became the *happily ever after* and my journey has been one of realizing that we are not merely meant to awaken *from* this world; we are here to awaken *to* it; *through* it. And for me, the key to this has been what I have come to call the loving freedom of holistic awakening, though there are numerous names – old and new – for it.

I came to realize that awakening doesn't transcend the world; it transcends the division within us. And I realized that the problem isn't duality, it's our unconscious belief that duality is inherently real. In fact, oneness that negates duality reinforces it, whereas that which embraces it is actually *holistically* non-dual.

This deeper understanding of oneness is better known as the Middle Way because we come back down from the mountain top into our hearts, our lives, and the world *as it is*. So awakening isn't just pure white light; it's the full spectrum rainbow diffuse with it, i.e. being, like love, is as much about relating *to* form as transcending it.

Life is Lila (the great cosmic play), not Maya (the great cosmic illusion). This richness of experience is what *being in the world but not of it* is really about. Transcendence *alone* is a copout, and transcendental love, like the idealized love of fairytales, is the booby prize.

However, since the same can also be said of the intellectual understanding of spiritual insights, I'd like to bring these ones down to earth by sharing more of my own story with you.

After a childhood engrossed in the study of spirituality and metaphysics, I spent several years traveling the world studying with traditional wisdom keepers and modern spiritual innovators. Sounds impressive or even romantic, right?

But to be honest, much of it was a pain in the ass. I kept at it because it served to deepen and expand upon an awakening to our non-dual nature I had in my early twenties – the non-abiding kind, i.e. the one that opens the door but not enough to get through.

In subsequent years, however, this prince transformed into a frog and the fairy godmother into the Furies as I tried to mould myself into what I thought an enlightened being should be rather than express the simple unconditioned truth of who I loved to be. Instead, I followed my spiritual bliss, believing that the loving luminous spaciousness of awareness was awakened love.

It was not.

Contrary to what many teachers of intention and awakening say, any psychologist will tell you doing so leads to dissociation, not abundance or realization, because when I crafted an idealized self I inadvertently sealed myself in behind the facade with the very negative core beliefs I was hoping it would protect me from. Then the vicissitudes of life came along and with ruthless compassion picked me apart until I had no choice but to let go or die of the pain.

Yet in the space created by this act of letting go, I rediscovered *being*, this time as an indestructible center and also as an incredible gratitude for the gift of life, even as it was tearing my heart out and my dreams apart.

That's the paradox; the mystery.

Life is a sharing between this person that is me and this vast Universe that is *also* me. It's the most incredible journey of self revelation and yet there's no self to grasp. And with that, there's a poignant beauty to suffering because there's no need for it... and yet there is.

And it's our receptivity to this that enables us to keep a foot in each world – one in life and the other in presence – and from there to commune with the Divine. Oneness means being open to anything arising in the present moment. Indeed, oneness is *what* it is because it is *what is*. So, it's true to what's *happening*, not to what's happiness.

With this opening came a profound sense of grace, of being blessed, and a melting into a love so intimate yet transcendental that it was more familiar to me than the very self I thought I was. But unlike my first awakening, this time it was okay to be my egoistic self too – without the need to try to fix or transcend it. I was perfect despite my imperfections. If anything, I was perfect, thanks to them in a *wabi-sabi* way.

I came to realize that love is never meant to keep us safe; it's here to help us remember ourselves by freeing us of ourselves. Love is the freedom *of* love, paradoxical though that may be, whereas *happily ever after*, even if it were genuinely possible, would be a gilded cage in comparison.

This loving freedom is not a happy ending. It's simply co-creation between what we want to experience in life and what this moment wants us to experience, and with that there's an outpouring of gratitude that anything exists at all.

This gratitude for life, exactly as it is, is the ground of abundance because everything is a gift given unconditionally through love. Abundance is always here, but we have to start loving ourselves unconditionally to receive its gifts.

This is why the higher octave of manifesting is *co-creation* through the law of *affinity* rather than attraction. Co-creation is a gift, not a power, born of sharing, not controlling; relating, not manipulating. It takes two – the personal me and the Universal me – to be holistically one.

Yet the greater part of this exchange always remains uncertain and unknowable because this is what keeps life's juices flowing and the great cosmic play of Lila going. This is what to awaken *to* the world, *through* it rather than *from* it, looks like from the other side; when we've transcended the divided world *within us* by rediscovering the loving freedom of holistic awakening.

It reminds me of the love story in the modern classic movies *Before Sunrise* and *Before Sunset*. I don't want to give too much away if you haven't seen them, though I highly recommend that you do. But suffice it to say, there are some interesting parallels between the exploration of love in these films and the exploration of oneness that I've tried to share with you.

Although in saying that, I'd like to bring a deeper dimension to these films that will illustrate holistic non-duality in a more vivid way by contrasting Maya (the world as the great cosmic illusion) with Lila (the world as the great cosmic play).

There's a famous analogy in spirituality that compares the dualistic world to a movie and non-dual oneness to the person watching it in the movie theater fully aware that it is just a projection of flickering lights upon a screen. Here, awakening means transcending one's identification with the story because it's merely an illusion.

Holistic non-duality goes a step further by re-engaging with the movie because it's our capacity to be enthralled in it; to identify wholeheartedly with the characters and make their stories, joys, and sorrows our own, feeling that it's all real yet all the while knowing it's not. This makes movie going so worthwhile.

Admittedly, there's a danger of us losing ourselves in the plot at times but this is not the same as us losing the plot of ourselves altogether – which is what actually makes it necessary for someone like the evil stepmother of Cinderella to step in as the catalyst for change.

Yet once we can stand again with a foot in the world of form and the other in the formless, what is there to fear in the story or, more to the point, who is there to lose in it? There's no Cinderella without the cinders; no movie without an audience; no formlessness without form. It's all holistically one... alas, this recognition calls on a maturity not found in fairytales.

I must also admit that I still spend more time lost in the plot than straddling both worlds, but I tend not to lose the plot of myself that much anymore. By no means am I awakened. I've still a long way to go, though a bridge or channel has opened to *awakened consciousness*.

This channel is open to all of us. I'm no different than you!

So, here's what I suggest you do. Firstly, stop taking the great traditional teachings about awakening as gospel – including what I've written in this chapter – and use them as pointers only. Since awakening is your natural state, you must already know it at a fundamental level and just need to remember that.

My first awakening came about through this, though my later ones were through traditional methods. One day I just started persistently asking myself, "What is this *thing* we call conscious experience?" I stuck with it until finally it dawned on me that existence is a complete mystery and with that, the natural state of being was revealed.

Remember, this too is only a pointer; you need to find what resonates with you. Although I found traditional teachings incredibly insightful, the back-to-basics approaches of modern awakened teachers like Tim Freke, Eckhart Tolle, Adyashanti, Guy Finley, Scott Kiloby, and Jeff Foster were the most helpful and transformative.

Secondly, you need to recognize that the ego is not the villain. If anything, it's the shadow that lights the way. By facing your demons you take your power back from the self-limiting beliefs that created them.

I tried unsuccessfully to do this many times during the years until eventually I was so beaten down by life that I surrendered to God's will for me and committed myself – come Hell or high water – to owning and healing my *shit*.

I genuinely felt I owed it to my immortal soul and chose to deal with this karmic inheritance consciously as best as I could rather than leave it to be faced as *external* fate by my future incarnations as my previous incarnations had left theirs for me.

To be honest, most self-help and manifesting techniques didn't work for me until I found those rare gems with a strong heart signature based on authentic self-love and the non-dual understanding of abundance. Those included healer-teachers Rhonda Britten, Robert Holden, Mary A. Hall, Sonia Choquette, Lisa McCourt, and Cheryl

Richardson. But again you need to find which approach and teachers resonate with you.

And finally, seize the moment. My journey has been a long one, but it needn't be for you. The planetary energy shift that's taking place right now is making it easier for us to resonate with the holistic awakened energies of intention, love, and oneness, and it's accelerating exponentially.

It's no coincidence that you're alive at this time reading this book. The Universe believes in you. I do too.

And so should you.

About the Author

Mark H. Kelly has a background in applied physics, software development, and ESL teaching, although his real passion has always been metaphysics and spirituality. Guided by the angels and ascended masters from an early age, he later spent several years on a spiritual odyssey traveling the world learning from traditional wisdom keepers and modern spiritual innovators.

Mark is certified in Reiki, pranic-healing, Shakti yoga, and Ayurvedic psychology and nutrition. He is also proficient in spiritual counseling, soul reading, spiritual astrology, tarot, meditation, energy healing, and NLP.

He is well versed in the Eastern spiritual traditions and was a student of Tibetan Buddhist Rinpoche Amni Trulchung of the Nyingma-Dzogchen lineage. He also studied shamanism and was a student of Wendy Luckey, a shaman-healer holding several Native American lineages.

Mark lives in Athlone, Ireland, but spends much of his time abroad. He is currently working on a book exploring holistic non-duality.

http://www.markhkelly.com

MY QUEST TO FIND TRUE LOVE: THE FUNDAMENTAL FIVE CONNECTIONS

Jasmin Terrany, LMHC

Like many New Yorkers in their twenties, dating took up a lot of my time. Because I was always fascinated by the process of finding *the one*, I developed a few principles that were integral in my dating journey.

Firstly, the type of person you are *attracted to* isn't necessarily *good* for you. Secondly, consider the fundamental five connections when *trying on* a potential partner. Thirdly, know yourself and what you *need*. It has been said, "Success is when preparation meets opportunity."

Surprisingly enough, I took this concept to heart in my quest to find true love.

What Are My Patterns?

The number of fashion models I've dated is just silly. Regardless of where I was or who I was with, if I was single and there was a gorgeous man in the room, it was *his* attention I wanted. He was my conquest. I would feel pride in myself when somehow my flirty eye-contact and shy smile would get him to walk his handsome self in my direction. When it eventually came out that he was, in fact, beautiful for a living, I added a check mark to the tally in my head.

Usually I'd date those fashion models for a bit. I'd follow my ego's quest to be unlike any other girl they'd ever known. I'd seem unimpressed by their physical beauty, be clear that sex wasn't something I shared with people I didn't love, and proceed to create a deep meaningful one-sided relationship. I'd ask them to share their deepest thoughts and feelings, and be a true, loving friend to them. Often

I'd become the person they would open the most to, the person they felt most comfortable to be themselves around, and, frequently, the woman with whom they thought they would like to spend the rest of their lives with forever.

I had it down to a science. I knew how to make men fall in love with me, and not just any men, but the attractive ones: the arrogant, too pretty for their own good, can-have-any-woman-they-want ones.

In my head, I was a superstar.

At that point, I hadn't yet realized my ego's game. I simply thought I was a loving person who wanted an attractive man. As my pattern persisted, I began to notice a deeper theme: these men usually knew very little about me, didn't try to know my soul, and rarely challenged me. It became clear that even though I may have been *their* best friend and ideal mate, they weren't mine. While momentarily satisfied by the catch, I ultimately ended up disappointed in the emptiness that ensued when I wasn't loved the way I needed to be.

After reflecting on my dating patterns, it became clear that the basis for which I chose my mates was fundamentally flawed. Was it possible that I was attracted to people who weren't what I needed? If I wanted a soul connection, *why did I choose men simply because they were good looking? And why did I end up as everyone's therapist?!*

Do I want to move beyond my patterns?

I started to journal about my meaning of true love. It became evident that I needed someone to understand who I was on the inside. I realized I needed someone to be my partner and best friend. I needed someone who challenged me to know myself more deeply. To find him, I would have to push myself outside my comfort zone, focus less on the superficial, and open my *own* heart to deeper connections: intellectual, emotional, and spiritual.

But was I ready?

What is the Universe Giving Me?

One day it happened. I met a guy who *saw* me. The ease and comfort I experienced in his presence was that of a deep connection. Yet, there was a catch. The exterior of this man was far from what I had been attracted to; the opposite in fact. He wore something on his head that I later found out was called a turban. Due to the cultural beliefs of his Sikh religion, none of his hair had ever been cut and his full beard was tied up under his chin. If that wasn't different enough, I soon found out that his family was morbidly obese. So this chubby guy in the turban was actually a hundred pounds less than he was before we met. Needless to say, this was not remotely close to the tanned, handsome, gym buffs I was accustomed to dating.

Despite those differences, I really liked him and we were instantly connected. Physically, however, he was nowhere close to what I had in mind for a partner. And to top things off, I had no idea how he would fit into my life.

Thanks Universe! Way to throw me a curve ball.

How can I open my heart to receive?

"Ok," I thought, "what do I need to learn?"

After some effort, I learned that my own insecurities about my body and attractiveness drove my desire to have a gorgeous man by my side. *If he is hot, it must mean that I am too, right?* It also turned out that my so-called *giving* pattern had less to do with loving and more to do with proving my own significance, not to mention a stellar way to avoid my own vulnerability.

Could I move beyond these tendencies? Could I allow a deep connection to take precedence over my ego's desire to be with an attractive man? Was I ready to be a vulnerable equal participant in a loving relationship? With a lot of soul searching and a big push outside my comfort zone, I finally opened my mind and heart for a relationship with this man; for four years in fact.

There I had it: a spiritual, emotional, intellectual, and now physical connection. I felt grateful that I had the courage to experience the depth of connection for which I had yearned for.

We both thought we were going to spend the rest of our lives together. However, a frustrating issue kept arising: lifestyle. Somehow, we just couldn't find a middle ground. The way he ate, drank, and lived his life just didn't mesh with the way I did things. He wanted to live in a home with his parents... *forever.* He was also committed to raising his sons in turbans. Despite respecting his family and culture, his vision of his future simply didn't align with mine. Tried as we could to compromise, it seemed that love and connection wasn't enough to make it work.

After much heartache and pain we decided to part ways, *neither of us willing to lose ourselves for the other.*

How can I access my truth?

Having struggled so much over the physical and lifestyle connections in that relationship, it was no surprise that a year later I found a man who perfectly matched my needs in these areas. It seemed that this *rebound guy* was the pendulum swing to the opposite extreme; not quite yet the perfect balance, but pretty refreshing nonetheless.

I connected both emotionally and physically with this new man, and his lifestyle couldn't have been a better match. But after having experienced such a strong spiritual and intellectual connection in my past relationship, I felt something was missing. I tried to make it work though. I tried really hard. He was completely perfect on paper and too good to lose. He was handsome, loving, kind, independent, wealthy, and he ate and exercised just like I did. And he absolutely adored me!

So what exactly was my problem? Was I asking for too much? Was there another deep-seeded issue that the Universe was forcing me to confront? More than a year later, after various breakup attempts, I realized I couldn't force the spiritual and intellectual connection I needed.

Fundamental Five Theory

After ending this relationship, I was back to what seemed like square one: single. In the process of becoming clearer about what I *didn't* want, I pushed myself to figure out what I *needed.* So I developed my theory of the Fundamental Five Connections:

1. Physical

2. Intellectual

3. Emotional

4. Spiritual

5. Lifestyle

I began to realize just how often people started relationships based on the excitement that comes from the fantasy of the potential mate. Or in the beginning they connect in one or a few of these five connections. However, after some time, if all five connections are not satisfied, many people are often left wondering what went wrong.

I noticed that when talking about a new love interest, people often describe external assets: what they do, what they look like, what their family is like, and so forth. Focusing on the external often prematurely turns people *on* or *off,* i.e. he's a doctor and loves kids! We're perfect for each other!

As important as the external assets can be, an equally, if not more important, question to ask is: who is this person in relation to me? What is our actual connection like? Do we connect in some or all of the ways that are most important to me? I'm playing with the idea that *people need a certain level of connection in each of the following areas to create a solid foundation in a relationship.*

The Fundamental Five Ways to Connect with your Partner

1 **Physical**: Do we have good chemistry? Does it feel natural and enjoyable to be in the other's physical presence? Do I enjoy expressing myself with this person on a physical level (affection, sexuality, eye contact, etc.)?

2. **Emotional:** Can this person understand and handle my emotions? Do I feel comfortable sharing them? Can I be myself on an emotional level?

3. **Spiritual:** Does this person share and respect my spiritual and non-spiritual beliefs? Do I feel comfortable sharing them? Can I be myself on a spiritual level?

4. **Intellectual:** Can this person connect with me intellectually in a way that feels satisfying? Can I express myself on an intellectual level?

5. **Lifestyle:** If I had to adapt to or learn to accept their world (culture, morals, eating habits, sleeping patterns, cleanliness, social habits, humor, health, hobbies, etc.), would that be comfortable? Can I maintain the parts of my life that I value most?

How Can I Manifest my Needs?

This theory helped me define my needs in a partner and, through the process, I was able to know myself a bit better. But at that point, I realized I needed to pause. I had been through a lot over those years; the ups and downs of loving and losing. I needed to heal. All of this *trying to find a mate* didn't leave much room for me to deal with the pain, frustration, hurt, helplessness, and fear that I had been unconsciously burying deep inside.

I recognized that maybe *I needed to love me before I could find him*. I had gotten clear about what I wanted in a man, so then it was time to surrender it to the Universe. Now was the time to learn how to love and accept all of me. I wanted to accept my darkness and my light, to learn to be ok with my internal discomfort, and to stop seeking external sources for the quick fix. So I let myself spend a year with just me; I let myself cry myself to sleep on Saturday nights if that's what I needed. I let myself feel and lovingly accept my full human experience. I realized that if I couldn't accept all of me, how could I ever accept anyone else?

Eventually… it *actually* happened. I found my husband. I found the man who challenges my mind, tends to my heart, soothes my soul, gives me goose bumps with his kisses, and simply feels like home to me. Had I met him any sooner I wouldn't have been ready. The fact that I had gotten so clear about what I needed and who I was, made me ready when he appeared. Like they say: "Success is when preparation meets opportunity."

I'm just grateful I was prepared.

So now my journey of *being* in an everlasting relationship has begun…

About the Author

Jasmin Terrany, LMHC, is a licensed psychotherapist with two master's degrees in counseling from Columbia University and a bachelor's degree in Spanish Literature from Tufts University. Her life therapy private practice combines psychotherapy & life coaching with mindfulness & meditation. In addition to individual and couples therapy, she also runs groups, leads classes, workshops, and guest lectures.

Terrany's inspirational blog has garnered thousands of followers nationwide. Her specialties include developing self-love and confidence, improving relationships, releasing stress, anxiety and sadness, creating healthy relationships with food and body, uncovering life's purpose, and overcoming quarter-life crises.

Two of her deepest passions are travel and spiritual growth. She has spent time in over forty different countries and has focused much of her education on developing multicultural awareness and her own spiritual journey.

http://www.jasminbalance.com

THE LOVE PUZZLE

Nazee (Behnaz) Mirshamsi

Every night when I look at my own baby picture in my bathroom then look back at myself in the mirror, I feel truly loved and alive. This is an amazing connection between me and *myself*; my true essence and the person standing in front of the mirror. I can see my true self separate from my roles: being a mom, wife, child, relationship coach, friend, author, and speaker.

Placing myself into those innocent child's eyes, for a few silent moments I stay connected eye-to-eye in the mirror and embrace the child within me, loving myself unconditionally for who I am. I remind myself where I have come from and where I am going. I get connected to my higher Source, knowing that I am on Earth for a purpose.

> *I'm on a journey to my dream*
> *Learning, growing, teaching*
> *And most importantly*
> *Loving*
> *Seeing people as important as myself*
> *Loving all for who they are*
> *Finding the innocent inner child in everybody*
> *And accepting them as they are,*
> *Spread peace and love all around the world*
> *Love to live... live to love*

My journey started when I was looking for love and feeling that I was not getting enough. At the age of twenty-two, I got married to my beloved husband whom I had been admiring for a long time. At the beginning, everything was fine like any other marriage. The problem arose after a few months of not getting as much attention as I desired. I noticed that I was always demanding my husband's affections through the words *I love you.* After a while, I asked myself, "Why do I need his words? Why do I need his attention so much? Why am I so desperate for his hugs and admiration?"

One night, after an argument, hating myself for being so insistent and tired of fighting, I remembered my childhood. I was a very easygoing child and a gorgeous girl, mostly silent and shy, and sometimes very emotional. I couldn't remember being told *I love you* or being praised by my parents. I had never been told *I am proud of you,* never been hugged, and rarely been kissed, if ever.

As a child, I had never realized that lack of love and self-confidence. But in my married life, I recognized that even though I was aware of my parents love, deep down I still needed to hear it and feel the warmth.

That… was an enlightening night for me.

Firstly, as a mom, I came to understand how important it is to say *I love you* to my kids, to be around them, to listen to them, to understand them, and to praise them. Secondly, as a wife, and still a daughter, I thought, "I need to hear those words." So by being honest with myself, I started to *ask* and talk about my emotional needs with my husband and then with my mother. With some hesitation they started to express their love more openly.

My husband and I learned to share our dreams and desires with each other but there were still lots of disagreements and misunderstandings. I still felt empty and unloved because I did not believe I was a lovable person and I didn't love myself. As a result I couldn't believe in words of others when they told me they love me, either. Our relationship was going downhill.

A few years later, a new chapter in my life began *a journey to awareness.* Interestingly, my mom was the person who launched me on this voyage. She introduced me to some transformational books that changed my life. Now I realize how grateful I should have been, all along, for her wisdom and love. I started to believe in the power of words, thoughts, and dreams. I started to heal my anger and resentment with love. I started to send love and peace even to those who were irritating. As my father had taught me to *easily forget every sadness and hurt; forgive everybody and let it go,* I started to forgive everybody, including myself, for everything.

I was still looking for something more to do. Something inside me was urging me to create a difference, do things in a new way, and change people's lives. At first, I thought I needed a job. The cultural norm in my country was that a mother with small children did not work outside the house unless she really needed to. My husband preferred that I not work outside and stay at home with our young daughter and baby boy, but I kept on bringing up the idea that a job may help me.

One day, I was so tired of being opposed about my ideas of working, I left the house to have time alone in peace and reflect on my life's recent events. I was always inspired by nature, so I headed for my favorite hiking route in the mountains. As I was going up, my ears caught the sound of running water. I followed the sound and came to a small creek where I saw the water flowing over the rocks in it. Just by watching that scenery, I was inspired. The water was clear and some of the rocks were sharp and jagged. But there was no sense of conflict. The water just kept on flowing calmly, gradually turning those sharp corners on the rocks to softer shapes.

"Wow!" I thought to myself. "This is incredible! It is trying to speak to me. Rocks and water! Water with its flexibility, transparency, clarity, and persistence is living besides those hard stones and moving boundlessly." I had found inner peace and a solution to my relationship with my husband.

If there are people who are as rigid as the rocks in your life, you can still impact them with your flexibility, transparency, clarity, and persistence, just like the water. Without any conflict, you can continue on your way, get along with everybody, and be able to overcome every obstacle in your way with love.

Later that same week, I went for another walk down the street to fill a prescription at the pharmacy. A bookstand captured my attention. The books were all about health, which reminded me that I had some health booklets in English that would be helpful to young mothers. Since I had a BA in translation, I decided to translate them so I took the contact information of the publisher and contacted them, telling them that I would like to submit translations of their booklets. They contacted me back and accepted my translation. That event was a triumphant victory without a battle. I could stay at home with my children and at the same time be working. The power of love. Flowing instead of struggling.

Was I fulfilled? Not there yet. There was still something missing. I still didn't believe in myself, so I didn't continue on with more translation. There was also a small voice inside of me saying, "I am a unique, creative, and talented individual who has come to this world to make a difference." But I couldn't trust that voice. Besides, I didn't know how.

At about this time, my family moved to Canada. Right after landing, I participated in a transition workshop that helped me get to know myself better. I started acknowledging my positive past and building my self-confidence. I discovered that in order to feel fulfilled I needed to be in the service of others therefore I decided to become a life coach.

In the midst of professional training towards the goal of becoming a life coach, I continued to learn more about myself. My husband and I were not fighting anymore and our arguments wouldn't last. From time to time, I would get upset because I thought he did not respect me as much as I respected him. One night, at about 1 a.m., I fell into bed too exhausted to do anything at all, not even brushing my teeth. Shortly after, my husband came in, but he took time to brush his teeth, do his prayers, and brush his hair. I was wondering how he could do all these things even though I knew he was ready to collapse as well.

Seconds after this question, I had a revelation that answered a lot of my questions.

I had always wondered why my husband was more loved and respected than I was by others. I realized it was all because he respected and loved himself more than I did and he was committed to taking good care of himself.

If I was thinking that I was not receiving enough respect, it was because I was not respecting myself. If I was thinking that I was not receiving enough love, it was because I did not love myself. And if I was thinking nobody believed me, it was because I did not believe in myself.

That night had been a turning point in my life. Now I needed to figure out the next step: how to increase my self-love, self-respect, and self-belief. The pieces (notes/ word) of my love-puzzle (love-song) started to come together one piece (note/ word) at a time, each at the right time.

One night when I was going through my photo albums, I found a baby-picture of myself. I looked in her innocent eyes and then closed my eyes and embraced it inside of me. That beautiful little girl was still there, alive! I started talking to her. "Hey love, you have been unknown; but I am *knowing* you. God loves you and I love you. There is nobody out there that could understand you except God and me! Now I am here for you and I promise to take care of you from now on. Your life is a gift, unwrap it and share it with the world. I will support you and I will cheer for you. "

Using the childhood picture exercise and a mirror exercise helped me to get back to my true self, to my higher Source, and to people. I believe these are love principles: If you want to be fulfilled and loved, love yourself, love your higher Source, and love others.

> *Finally I have found love.*
> *You are love,*
> *You are who you are*
> *Think of this:*
> *When there are no roles left every night,*
> *You are still there, loved and safe*
> *Be grateful for all you have*
> *Be grateful for what you don't have*
> *Be grateful for your life*
> *Be grateful for each and every moment*
> *Be love, be peace, simply be you*
> *Love to live…Live to love*

Having this beautiful love-puzzle, now my journey continues even when there are unexpected bends in the road. When uncommon things happen during the stressful times, and while worries arrive, I should keep an eye on each action, each thought and each conversation and remind myself of my choices. I ask myself, "Is this choice in alignment with my new awareness and the following love principles?"

Love yourself, love God, and love others.

I need to constantly keep my balance with practicing, meditating, praying, learning, and growing. I need to remind myself that every day is offering me a variety of choices that, ultimately, I can choose to either create peace and love, or to create hatred and conflicts inside and out.

My nightly exercise, meditation, and praying have become precious tools in my everyday life. Now I am in deeper connection with my higher Source and myself. I have become truly loving to others, and have fewer expectations. I can easily say, "I love you" and I really mean it.

It's our choice, let's choose to live with love.

About the Author

Behnaz (Nazee) Mirshamsi is a life-long learner who sees every situation and every individual as an inspirational teacher in her life.

She is a certified professional co-active coach from CTI, trained and mentored by Jack Canfield (co-author, *Chicken Soup for the Soul* series and America's #1 success coach). She focuses on love and relationship in her work. She is also a health and wellness trainer.

She is passionate about coaching and loves to empower people in finding their life purpose and inspire them. Through out her life experiences, education, learning, failing, and recovering, she has learned a lot. She is knowledgeable about relationships, overcoming obstacles, living gratefully, boosting self-confidence and love. She accepts and respects all people the way they are. She believes that every individual is here for a reason. Her work includes one-on-one coaching, e-courses, teleconferences, and leading transformational workshops.

http://www.coach2love.com

A SMILE WILL SET YOU FREE

Heather Price

Have you ever felt so overburdened where every moment is painful and even breathing becomes an effort?? Where there seems to be no light; no window of opportunity; no optimism?

This is the illusion of separation: when you feel separated from your core essence, and from the Universal heart that unites us all.

It is important to understand separation and the re-connection to your true nature and Universal heart. Understanding those will help create the opportunity for you to walk more authentically, confidently, and consciously on the earth. I hope to demonstrate what an impact the perception of separation can have by sharing a time of darkness and fear in my personal journey and then I will leave you with some ideas and tools to consider using on your journey. These tools have assisted me to reconnect with, and be energized by, my own inner light, and to open my heart fully to the love of the Universal heart that unites us all.

Living Honestly in Awareness

Although now living a life illuminated by a loving connection with the people I walk with and serve, and with the Universal heart, there have been a number of times in my life when I have felt completely alone and separate from everyone and everything.

One of the most challenging times was when I experienced a significant disruption in my capacity to create financial wealth and stability in my life, even though I felt abundant in every other way. This was exacerbated when, out of the blue, my health was threatened by a severe fall and I struggled every day with pain and the fear that I may not recover. No matter what I did, I simply could not bring enough light into my life to balance the darkness I was feeling.

At my lowest point, I stopped *thinking* about my experience and, instead, began to *feel* where my experience was manifesting in my body, understanding the power of bringing the darkness of my mind into the healing light and love of my heart-space. At first my body ached with fear and then it became tense as I panicked with a feeling of helplessness. Finally, it sagged with grief. I felt like an animal in a dark hole unable to claw my way out. However, there was some relief in being able to validate what I was going through in my heart. This enabled me to identify and understand the feeling of what I was going through and find compassion for myself, instead of self-condemnation.

While I kept the depth of my burden to myself, I did seek help on a physical level, and found some emotional support and relief through sharing with close friends that I was financially and spiritually going through a difficult time. However, the depth of my despair, and my feelings of shame around the position I was in, was not something I could share with anyone. My silence allowed the darkness inside me to grow unchecked, and it felt like there was no turning back, and no way to go forward. Although I often felt trapped and depleted, I attempted to trust what I was going through, and prayed that there would be a time when the pain in my body would pass. All this time, the Universal heart continued to hold a loving space for me.

A Smile Breaks Through

One day when I was feeling particularly low, I took the time to sit and fully feel my experience and to write down what I was going through, bringing it to light, instead of keeping it inside of me.

At that time of feeling in the grip of separation, a smile came from deep inside and rose to the surface. I remember everything I was feeling coming to a stop in that moment, and I suddenly became aware of the sound of my son sawing a tree branch in the garden. Then a bird called out sharply, as if to remind me to breathe. As welcomed air flowed into my depleted lungs, I saw a flash of a blue ocean in my mind, and for a brief moment I felt connected with nature, and the love that I have for the earth and her creatures. I even heard the words *you are loved* whispered in my ear, coming from deep inside myself.

The Emergence of Truth

Little by little, I felt the urge to merge back into life, and began an honest dialogue with myself that included taking a look at what was good in my life at that moment. It went something like this: "I am stuck and depleted of energy right now. However, I still have a roof over my head, decent clothes to wear and food to eat. I am blessed to have family and friends who care about me. I am loved. Smile, relax, open your heart, breathe deeply, and be present."

Then, a persistent voice spoke from a deeper place: "I am afraid; I am powerless over my life."

And a lighter voice replied: "But my life is not over. I am breathing, my heart is beating, and I can still feel."

I remember, at that very moment I was bitten by an ant on my left elbow. Ants mean many things to me; they are persistent, hard-working team players. And yet, I find myself getting annoyed with their insistence in being where they are not welcome. Like negative thoughts, they will take over if you don't do something about them.

The dialogue continued after the ant bit me: "Every thought has the potential to add to my energy tank, or to deplete it; it is my choice... the thought of love adds energy immediately, fear loses energy instantly, rage consumes a massive amount of energy. Open, honest expression will set you free."

Trust Box

In that moment, I knew I had a choice to bring energy into or out of my energy tank, and I thought of my trust box where I have stored the most magical moments in my life, like when my childhood dream of being a mother finally became a reality; a tiny butterfly attached itself to my third eye for half a minute while I was searching for a new pathway for my life; Mother Earth spoke to me for the first time; I was channeled guidance in Hawaiian language during a spiritual quest to Hawai'i.

Illumination

As healing light began to fill my energy tank at last, I found myself saying out loud, "I am loved and blessed in so many ways, in this and other worlds. I am a powerful being of light and I make a difference to the world every day. I know what my gifts are, and I have clear visions and dreams. I know who I am and where I have come from. I know that I feel like I am separated from Universal flow right now, and that this is an illusion and that I am never out of Universal flow. I know that this too will pass, but this too is Divine, and if I let go of my fear, a door will open to the miracles that happen every day. I know that everything is energy and has a living spirit. I know I am connected to everything in the Universe, and I am a powerful manifester of love and light when I choose to be."

Transformation

Over the next few weeks the love and light that I consciously created through being fully present and loving with myself attracted more of the same energy, and abundance began to flow into every area of my life. My health improved rapidly as I surrendered my fear and transformed it into faith. My heart filled with all the love and support I had around me. My mind searched for ways to be optimistic at every opportunity. My spirit soured with creativity, and my trust in my capacity to manifest grew. I knew that I had whatever I needed to not only survive, but to thrive! There was also a deeper realization, that I could never be separated from Universal flow, or the Universal heart that unites all of creation, and that was I was experiencing was separation from my faith in myself, and trust in my journey.

There are five suggestions I have to help you prepare for times when you may experience the illusion of separation.

1. Walk Strongly in the World

Knowing who you are, where you are from, and where you are going will help you walk strongly in the world. Take the time to become conscious of what builds your energy tank and be mindful that your thoughts are energy, and have the potential to harm or heal. It is wise to get into the habit of keeping your energy field clean at all times and to fill it with light and joy by expressing gratitude for the countless blessings that come your way.

Write a list of the things that fill you with love and light energy; the natural gifts you have to offer the world; and the ways you feel you are being true to yourself and making a difference.

2. Build a Trust Box

Compile a list of at least three magical experiences you have had and will help you to remember the abundance and support of the Universe. Put these memories into your internal Trust Box, so that you can turn them at any time to remind you to trust in yourself and your journey. Your Trust Box will also assist you to believe in your dreams, and to trust in your capacity to manifest them.

3. Smile and Breathe Deeply at Every Opportunity

The healing power of your breath is enormous. Combine your smile with your breath and you will create radiant energy immediately. Try smiling at yourself in the mirror, or when you are meditating or walking. It is natural to smile when you hear a child laugh or a bird sing or when you think of or greet someone you love. Smile at every opportunity, and remember to breathe your smile in and then to breathe it out to the world.

4. Be Grounded and Present

Learn to be present with your *self* and your experiences. When you are grounded, you feel strong and in your power. Take time to fully notice what is happening around you and build your skills as an observer. Practice moving in and around situations rather than being in the middle of them, and stand confidently in your power rather than give it away. This is how you connect with, and be in alignment with, your high self, which will assist you to make clearer and more balanced decisions in your life.

5. The Continuing Journey:

I've shared my own experience of separation and reconnection here with you to demonstrate ways you can consciously create loving connection with the Universal heart at every opportunity, and to be prepared for times of disconnection and adversity.

It is simple really: *remember that everything is energy, and when you learn to keep your focus on consciously building your energy tank through trust, gratitude, self-love, and optimism, you will be free to walk lightly, lovingly, and in awareness, on this precious earth.*

About the Author

Heather Price is a social scientist, a shamanic healing practitioner and trainer, and a creative counselor. She guides people from all walks of life, and is passionate about supporting the communities she belongs to.

Heather is the global leader for the Vision Team for The Difference, a global community project united in their quest to make a difference by creating love and joy, to open and heal humanity's heart. She is a published author, and writes a regular on-line column, *Spirit in Life and Business*, for *LivingNow* Magazine. As host for *WAKE UP with Heather Price* radio, a branch of the The Difference™ Radio Network, Heather aspires to inspire people to walk consciously and gently on the earth. She sees herself as earth woman, mountain dweller, visionary and dream-holder. You can find out more about Heather and her work, or connect with her via her website.

http://www.heatherprice.net

TRUE LOVE GROWS FROM WITHIN

Althea de las Estrellas

*And the day came when the risk to remain tight in a bud
was more painful than the risk it took to blossom.*
~Anais Nin~

It is hard for one to feel good about oneself in today's society. The media has completely taken over global culture. No matter who we are or where we grew up, we are constantly bombarded with messages that encourage the painful awareness of the gap between where we are and where we are told *we should be*. We've all been dealing with it to a greater or lesser degree, consciously or not, since a very young age.

For the sake of living up to the standards the media and society set for us, a lot of us are in constant emotional pain. We suffer, we struggle to accept ourselves, and we don't know who we *really* are or what we *really* want from life. But we sure know what we are supposed to want, so we usually end up striving for that, even if it ends up making us miserable.

It's easy to feel hopeless in this society, but there are also more teachers now than ever before putting powerful and positive messages out into the world, showing and telling us. "There is another way. You don't have to live this way. You don't have to resign yourself to a life of suffering and struggle. You have options. You can be happy. You can feel good about yourself. You can create the life of your dreams. It is possible."

The Challenge

I was a very happy little girl. Like most little kids, I tremendously enjoyed myself just living life, taking every experience as an adventure to be enjoyed to the fullest. It was very easy to love myself back then. I liked who I was and was really self-confident. That is: Until my perception of myself started to be dramatically influenced by the people and the culture surrounding me. Eventually came a point when I looked solely to society and the standards set by the media to define myself as a person.

Yet I lived my childhood in a pretty diverse set of environments. I was a *serial exchange student,* meaning I did it five times and lived with eight different families across three different countries between the ages of twelve and seventeen.

In an attempt to successfully fit in with every family I lived with, I tried to apply the same formula I had applied with my own real family: Figure out what they want from me and become it, give them all I've got in hopes of getting their approval, love, and affection. I thought if everyone was happy with me, I'd be happy with myself as well.

The families I was trying to fit into (including my own) were radically different from each other; not just from different countries and cultures and languages, but also with different family models, beliefs, religions, values, dynamics, goals, aspirations, rules... and a *long* etc.

In each exchange program I was trying to become the person my surroundings *required* me to be.

The most powerful lesson I learned from these experiences was that I could not stand on my head in enough ways to please them all. I would lose my mind and myself in the process.

By age nineteen, I had already lived years of feeling totally and absolutely worthless, in part because of my inability to create all the love I desired through what I understood to be the only method: gaining others' approval and affection.

Great things happened in my life. I found life-changing love, I was blessed to have an amazing therapist for a couple of years who helped me a great deal, and I overcame a lot of my fears. Some of my biggest struggles remained, however. Self-hatred was a seed I planted deep within me at a very young age and it continuously grew until it almost destroyed everything that ever felt good in my life. And to overcome it I had to pull it out of my consciousness from the roots.

This self-hatred manifested itself in many painful ways throughout my teenage years, whether through depression, insomnia, eating disorders, or self-harm. I would put myself in very unsafe and harmful situations without much regard for my own well-being.

I felt totally hopeless about the future and the only thing that kept me going was the feeling that there must be something more to life. Something I hadn't been exposed to yet.

I was painfully aware of the fact that most people around me were not happy, but they had sort of *gotten used to it* or had maybe given up. They were all coping the best they could, but I often wondered if things like happiness and fulfillment were just myths, something only talked about in movies, novels, and poems.

I felt really unmotivated to pursue any typical goals. I knew what I was supposed to want by society's standards. I felt guilty that I was lucky enough to have access to the possibility of achieving all of it, yet wanted none of it.

All I wanted was to feel happy, free, and fulfilled. I wanted to heal myself and get over my issues. I didn't care about going to college or getting a really good job. At that point, all I really knew was that in order for me to survive and keep going with life, I needed to strive for happiness and fulfillment.

I knew that for my life to be better, I needed to start feeling better. That was all I cared about.

How We Got Here

We all want love in our lives. Love is an integral part of being a human being. We all need attention, affection and support.

According to Maia Szalavitz in her Huffington Post article: "'Failure to thrive' in human infants has been shown to result from lack of individualized, nurturing, physically affectionate parental care, whether in an orphanage or due to extreme parental neglect. Babies' brains expect that they will experience nearly constant physical touch, rocking, and cuddling: without it, they just don't grow."

As mammals, that's how important love is to us. The Beatles said it and they were right: "All you need is love."

The question then is: How do we go about manifesting that love in our lives?

Most of us grew up being inadvertently taught to look for love outside of ourselves and that love equals approval. That's why so many of us spend our whole lives looking for outside approval as a way to satisfy our never ending desire and need for love. But as the old adage goes: you can't love others or fully receive their love if you don't know how to love yourself.

When you don't fully accept who you are and love yourself for it, when you define yourself and your worth based on how you rank on the scale of society's standards, you miss out on yourself and what you truly have to offer. You miss out on what makes you special, and on what makes you *you*.

And the world is missing out too.

How to Change

The beginning of self-love after years of self-hatred isn't easy. For a long time, I wanted to love myself. But I didn't know how to make it happen. It took a lot of introspection and time alone with myself to become aware of the sources of my self-hatred. It took a lot of effort and consistency to turn those negative beliefs on their heads and *re-program* myself with better ones.

I had to understand that because it took me years to develop the bad habits that got me to that terrible feeling place, it would take a while to radically change my inner workings and heal.

Up until then, I hadn't ranked self-love very high in my priorities. My prioritizing of pleasing others overrode my prioritizing of being good to myself more often than not.

Once I was able to be totally honest with myself, I realized that a lot of my core values actually made it impossible for me to love and accept myself as I was. I had internalized the idea that I was not

150

enough in and of myself and needed to be fixed and improved to be acceptable, even to myself.

After years of working on my self-esteem I finally surrendered and opened my heart, in essence, to myself. I decided that I cared more about my well-being and happiness than about some damn standards I internalized from society or my past. Finally, in a moment of total clarity I fully realized why loving and accepting myself had seemed such a difficult endeavor for so long.

I was trying to love myself from a place of dissatisfaction. I couldn't really love myself while I was still giving so much of my energy and attention to molding who I was to obtain the approval of those surrounding me.

I had two powerful streams going on in opposite directions. I needed to start loving myself the way I already was. Despite what others wanted from me or their reactions to my new approach to life. You can't be truly happy when you are fulfilling someone else's idea of happiness rather than your own.

I needed to let go of all of my past beliefs and start living my life from the premise that who I naturally am is a gift to this world and to myself, and it is my destiny to bring it out and share it with all who can appreciate it and benefit from it.

Letting go of that impulse to bully myself into *being better* whatever that meant and being what others wanted from me was a complicated and slow process for me. But, little by little, thought by thought, moment by moment, I brought myself to a different feeling place in time.

Things To Remember

The more you love and appreciate yourself for who you are, the more you reveal to yourself and to the world the treasure you truly are, and the more good others can take from your existence.

As you do this, it will become easier to appreciate others also for who they truly are instead of holding them to standards neither you nor them can live up to.

Change is possible. Allow yourself to relax and dare to let go of your fears. Open your heart and mind. Divorce yourself from all the beliefs that have gotten you to that dark place, where you don't love yourself, where you aren't there for yourself, and where you aren't living your life for you. Turn it around. Make a commitment to yourself: to help yourself feel better everyday and to learn to love yourself.

Here are the most important things to keep in mind in this journey:

- Be patient, forgiving, and kind with yourself.

- Give the least attention possible to your old negative patterns. Even when you find yourself engaging in them once again, don't dwell on it. Just move on to a better feeling way of doing what you are doing.

- Make an effort to consistently think of better thoughts about whatever you are going through to make things easier and better for yourself.

- Abstain from internal criticism and soothe yourself instead, whenever it comes up.

- You know you are on the right path when you feel better than you did before. It's that simple.

- We prioritize a lot of things in our lives that neither make us happy nor lead to our happiness.

Being happy is an everyday labor of love for yourself. It's an endless, moment to moment process of prioritizing what is best for you and feels better to you.

You can be happy and love yourself if you allow yourself to make it your number one priority. Do it. You are worth it!

About the Author

Althea de las Estrellas is a witchy twenty-something year old writer, designer, artist, and entrepreneur from Madrid, Spain. She is fully bilingual and spent a significant part of her life living in the US which has greatly influenced who she is today. Her passions include learning, art, pop culture, business, spirituality, branding, hip-hop and the evolution of consciousness. She is the founder and CEO of several companies. Amongst them, Lira in Wonderland: an arts and crafts supply and lifestyle online brand and Explicit Brand Design: a branding, graphic design, and marketing services firm.

Her main focus is to empower and inspire individuals and collectives to be all they can be through her varied mediums and services. In her personal life, she is completely devoted to her passions, husband, and pets.

http://www.altheadelasestrellas.com

THE GODDESS WHO ATTRACTED A NOBLEMAN

Colleen Hoffman Smith

The Goddess *rises up from the center of the open heart like a flower that unfolds with the warmth of the morning sun.*

The Nobleman *rises up from the center of the open heart like the wind that shifts out the storm and moves in the summer breeze.*

How can we have a chance to create healthy, loving relationships if we have no idea what is separating us from feeling authentic love? Some of us never had healthy role models. Our childhood experiences and interactions with our parents are imprinted in us. If we had parents who were unavailable, numbed out, addicted to substance, mentally unstable, or abusive, we now have a chance, in our present life, to shift our personal conflicts and emotional barriers that are connected to the wounded child.

Mom and Dad were a very attractive couple. With faith and dedication, they created their family; triplet daughters and a son. Their love of life and of their children taught us about the outer appearances and what was important to achieve success with family values. They did their best with what they knew.

Life burdens and financial struggles shut down communication between my parents. Their fears and self–doubt triggered stress. Mom and Dad didn't know how to emotionally take care of themselves and we felt their closed hearts with resentment. They blamed one another and we walked on eggshells becoming good children for love.

Mom was always the picture of a Goddess, yet inside she had depression and anxieties. Her love for her family was more important but her love for herself was blocked. With her diagnosed bipolar illness, medication attempted to remedy her chemical make-up but it numbed her feelings. Deep rooted pain kept her separated from love.

Eventually, Alzheimer's took her away from us.

Dad's noble character always looked out for his family. Early retirement brought him financial stress, emotionally separating him. His body started to break down with heart attacks and strokes. His physical suffering took him to his emotional past. In his last few years of life, Dad slowly let go of control and he forgave himself and others. His transparent heart revealed the Nobleman that he was.

My parents were great teachers, as I experienced their love and pain. I wanted to continue taking care of my emotional body so that I could be authentic, compassionate, peaceful, physically healthy, and unconditionally loving. Dramas and relationships continued to ignite fear, anger, self-doubt, resentment, disappointment, grief, guilt, and shame.

This negativity acted as a barrier to love. Every time I took responsibility and released the ignited pain, my presence that connected to my open heart deepened. I would crave for this feeling of peace. I called this presence the Goddess connection and my intention was to find out how to live this way. I realized that once I learned how to connect to this presence in me, I had a chance to attract a man who lived it… he would be a Nobleman.

Movies gave me a glimpse of the Goddess or the Nobleman. I gravitated to men and women on the big screen who had a presence of connected love and self-worth. I also experienced myself and relationships as I watched actors who were betraying and dishonoring each other. Life was like a movie as I observed people around me. How I responded or got triggered and how others reacted and behaved opened my eyes to clarity.

I would like to share my story and illustrate how I found the Goddess in me and attracted a Nobleman. I thought this type of relationship only existed in movies or dreams.

Each of my significant past partners took me to the same void that lived in me. I would feel abandoned, disrespected, betrayed, hurt, and angry. With them, I would have feelings of not being good enough and unloved. I continued to love, care, give, and be everything I *thought* they wanted... waiting for love to return.

After the failure of my second marriage and the end of another significant relationship, I found myself putting all of the same unhealthy energy into my career. I kept looking for fame and money to fill my void... until I crashed.

Sometimes in our lives we hit rock bottom and experience what we call *Hell*. For all of us it is dark, tough, and devastating. As we *break down*, we have the opportunity for *a breakthrough*.

This was the sequence of my *Hell* over three months.

- My second marriage failed.

- My business failed and went bankrupt.

- My youngest daughter left me to live with her dad.

- My health deteriorated (heart attack and cancer issues).

- My financial security was gone.

I felt... fear, anger, loneliness, judgment, and lack of self-worth.

Who was I?

A terrible mother... an undesirable woman... a failure. I was broken. It was like falling off a bridge into darkness; falling out of my mind, losing everything, and hating myself in the process.

I went into the closet in my room. I closed the door, curled up in a ball, and wept. I cried from the depths of my being for hours.

I surrendered... and chose to live!

I saw how these events changed me. My perceptions were being shattered. From this place in *Hell*, I started to rebuild my own foundation with faith, faced all my greatest fears, became humble, and started my journey back to my heart. I desired to be healthy in every part of my life with my mind, body, and spirit.

I found a way to let go of my resentment and unloving experiences. This took time, commitment, and practice. I peeled away layers of old skin that held darkness and I received the lightness of emotional freedom. My *inner workout* process took me to a place within that allowed me to see the lies that were planted in me. Feelings that I was not good enough or unworthy of love started to dissolve as I took responsibility, stopped blaming my relationships, and forgave my past. Once I let go of negative thoughts, I was able to switch on my heart-light.

I had no idea what beloved love was until feelings of self-worth, joy, peace, and self-love seemed to be running through my veins. Seeing others without judgment and not criticizing myself created a sacred space in me.

The Goddess had arrived!

I remember a day when I was walking on the beach, feeling my longing for partnership. I looked over during sunset and saw a man and woman who had to be in their 90's, dressed in evening attire. She was in a gown and he was in a tuxedo. As the sunset inflamed the beach and calmed the waters, this beautiful, beloved couple waltzed to their inner music. What a magical sight as I sat alone with my hope and watched them dance. I knew that was what I wanted: to grow old with someone and dance on the beach of my life.

Three months later, I was in the departure lounge at Toronto Pearson Airport. During my flight delay, a friendly man came up to me and started a conversation. I didn't recognize the Nobleman at first and I didn't know that he was the one, but I did feel him so different than any other man. I was drawn to his presence. As he boarded the plane, he asked for my number. As we said good bye, we held the moment that we knew was divine.

Bruce was this gentleman. When we started dating I was like a deer in the head lights. My past pain with other men had developed an over protective heart, but Bruce created a safe place for me to carefully open to truth and intimacy. One evening, Bruce held my hand and, as I looked into his ocean-blue eyes, he said that he would be patient,... waiting for me to open to him... as long as it took. That night, I melted in the arms of his trusting heart.

The Nobleman had arrived!

Together we discovered how to weave this sacred connection in our hearts, in our relationship, and with our children and families. It was the beginning of a new life.

This is an invitation to connect to the Goddess and Nobleman presence. Uncover the ingredients that create this connection in all of us. When you forget who you are or who they are, take my hand in these words and fall in love.

Who is the Goddess?

The Goddess is connected to her own empowered essence. She is attractive because she doesn't wear her pain for the world to see. She is not a victim or bully, and there are no *shackles of control* or power-struggle...

She has forgiven her past.

She takes care of her emotional body and allows her heart to open. Her wisdom comes from past experiences.

The Goddess inspires truth in the way she lives authentically. Her fear is held with compassionate understanding. She expresses without judgment and lives in the moment. She melts the armor around her heart.

Feel the strength of her softness.

Her eyes see the magnificence of you, beyond your pain. She listens because the information you are sharing is important, yet she knows her boundaries.

She hears you because she is aware and conscious of herself. She recognizes your talents and lifts them up in her heart. When you are with her you feel safe to be all that you are and she reveals herself to you as an equal. Her genuine nature creates a transparency for truthful dialogue.

The Goddess will take you by the hand with gentle kindness and here you have the choice to recognize this connection is in you.

Who is the Nobleman?

The Nobleman lives his manhood with gentleness and humble strength. He creates a sacred place for truth to be revealed. He takes care of his own demons and fights them to their death, releasing them to the heavens.

He lives with his head and heart connected and when he is not, he returns to his practice. His eyes of love come from his connection deep within.

The Nobleman loves with purpose and integrity. His leadership is inspiration instead of control. He is respected because he has no greed, his ego is tamed. He walks with confidence because his self-worth is strong. He is a brother to all of your friends, and a loving father role to all of the children. He will never blame or judge anyone; you are accepted and loved.

Communication for the Nobleman is intimate and truthful. He has no secrets and nothing to hide. You can feel that he adores you as no other. His open heart inspires you. He initiates thoughtfulness and tender caring for your needs. He lifts passion carefully in the beating of his heart. He knows just when to take you to new places and when he doesn't know, he asks. He sees the sun when your tears close your heart, honoring the darkness.

He recognizes peace because it lives inside him, uplifting the moments when you need a sense of humor.

You know that he is a Nobleman because when you look into his eyes, you can see his soul.

Remember the Nobleman. He desires to live in every man.

Love and Oneness Reflected

Find a way each day to take care of your negative feelings and move into beloved love connecting and reflecting the Nobleman and Goddess. When the Goddess joins together with the Nobleman, they are already ignited and connected to their own fire, with passion moving through their bodies.

Male and female energies take the lead when one or the other is needed. Each is in both and oneness is realized. This is a powerful union.

About the Author

Colleen Hoffman Smith is an author, facilitator, and developer of The Inner Workout Process which she created as her emotional support system. She has been sharing this powerful life practice for over fifteen years empowering others to experience a life of emotional freedom. This inspired Colleen to write her first book, *Pocket Guide to your Heart*.

Her connection of beloved love with her husband, Bruce, moved Colleen to share her relationship expertise in her next book, *Pocket Guide to your Heart for Relationships. The Inner Workout... The Bridge to Emotional Fitness,* is her most comprehensive work yet – a complete guide supporting one's journey to inner peace and self-worth.

Colleen also facilitates seminars and workshops worldwide and has certified and trained a team of inner workout coaches.

Colleen lives in Toronto, Canada, with her beloved husband, Bruce. Their beautiful children and grandchildren live close by.

http://www.colleenhoffmansmith.com

BECOMING A VESSEL: LIVING YOUR BLISS

Jeanine Nicole

A month ago, I was let go from my job. Literally, I was *let go*, and in the process, given my freedom. I had been working in a position that did not align with my purpose, but I began to grow comfortable in the role for the security it provided me. I did not dare unplug myself from such a source of stability, so I spent months feeling vapid from a predictably *safe* but reliable lifestyle.

As soon as I heard the news that I would be *moving in new directions*, immediately there was nervousness, excitement, fear, and relief. I had defied the call to adventure for so long, but at last the time had come and I had no other choice. In this moment, I was finally given the permission that I wouldn't give myself: to follow my bliss and be everything that I wanted to be.

I define my bliss as the circumstance when what I do is aligned with who I am and what I believe. All of a sudden, within a month of being let go, I went from a life filled with routine administrative tasks to a bustling life of teaching yoga, creating personal growth work-shops, and developing a bliss coaching program. In the process, I felt an empowerment and centeredness I had never known before.

Though evidence that following my bliss could be *successful* by societal standards had not yet appeared, still I gained confidence that there was nothing else I could or should do. Nothing else would create the success I so desperately sought: a life of integrity where I could share my gifts freely, shine brightly, and inspire myself and others along the way.

Throughout this process, I learned to surrender to the *highest good*, even if I didn't know what that was. My highest good was something that I often lost touch with, was unaware of, and could barely fathom. Many times, I even got in my own way in the very effort to grasp uselessly at what I believed to be my highest good.

In the end, attaining the best for our lives simply boils down to listening and love. We all want to love, be loved, and *be* love in the world, but the interplay of our humanity and our divinity can frequently be a rocky terrain. The more we learn to tune in and to receive, the more we can learn to follow the call towards our highest good. Following are four key lessons I learned along the way.

Lesson 1 – Become Ready and Available for the Best Possible Thing!

"I am available to more good than I have ever experienced, imagined, or realized before in my life"
~Rev. Michael Beckwith~

For a month, I internalized these words. They leapt from my heart right onto my lips each day. I saw their power burn holes through an old life and render me new in every fresh moment.

Two days after I received a transformative energy healing, upped my meditation practice from ten minutes a day to forty, and repeated the prayer quoted above with all my heart each morning, the miracle occurred: I lost my job and was released into a new horizon.

Ten minutes later, I was already on the go. I called up a contact who had recently interviewed me for a position at a yoga studio and I felt myself shaking in fear as I picked up the phone. I had already turned this position down, so what if the opportunity was lost? And if it wasn't, the job was based on weekend shifts, so how was I to pay my rent? All the fears were close to consuming me until I remembered the quote above and silently repeated it one more time.

Suddenly, I found myself in a state of grace and prayed simply for the best possible thing. I was open for this wish to manifest in a greater way than my fears or even my hopes. Five minutes later, I had not only secured the original shifts, but was also offered three extra shifts at a brand new yoga studio as part of an amazing community.

In the end, the situation of being sternly nudged to re-create my life taught me so much. It taught me that we often get in our own way with fear-filled stories that keep us from fulfilling our goals. It taught me that we are often so seduced by the comfort of the status quo that we pass up opportunities that would enable us to shine. It taught me that risks are indeed scary, but that the rewards are triple the price. And it taught me that while not everything is ever stamped as an official and ultimate *success*, a life filled with faith will carry us through the journey with an ease unlike any other.

Indeed, thanks to my internal shift from an approach of scarcity to one of abundance, I was newly living my gifts freely – I was loving life, and it was loving me back.

Lesson 2 – Accept your Humanity, Embrace your Divinity: Surrender to What Is

If everything was going so swimmingly, then why did I find myself on the twenty-fifth night, with hot tears spilling down my cheeks, stinking of jealousy, anger, and confusion? A heap of hatred so removed from my prior humility, I was embarrassed to even witness this dark side of myself: the part that grasps so clingingly and aches so longingly that it becomes frustrated and impatient.

That is the aspect of myself that only knows scarcity and whose fear swells uncontrollably, creating dark red dashes across the once blank canvas of a peaceful mind. My desperate desire to become a published writer, my competitive streak, and my inner hunger were manifesting as a sort of starvation that countered all the trust and bliss that I had been feeling just moments before.

We each have our own way of dealing with our shadow sides. Sometimes we choose distraction. Sometimes it is tears or a punching bag. Often, a few deep breaths will restore a small sense of calmness to a bleeding heart. For me, it is the page that softens me when I am in the stream of passion or despair.

That night, as I began to write, I became gentler with myself. I started to forgive the imperfections in my soul, the flaws within my heart, and the limitations of this life as an embodied being. That was just one of many moments where I knew I must cradle myself like a tender infant, knowing that self-hatred only doubles the pain and that self-love assuages any wound no matter how inconceivably great.

After some time, I returned to a peaceful sense of gratitude, knowing that I already carried all the seeds of what I longed for. My jealousies became indications of my innermost desires and even my potential.

Though they seem undesirable, these instances are the very moments when all the walls of the ego come crashing down, allowing you to rebuild your self, and your life. These are the times when all the resistance that has been building up melts all at once, relinquishing its stubborn need to control. There is a grace that comes in these moments when we accept our whole selves, not just the good likable parts.

When we learn to love our true selves, it becomes instantly easier to love others for their whole selves as well.

Lesson 3 – Ask for the What; Trust in the How

Though some would describe me as a free spirit, my need to control things sometimes eats me up from the inside out. The origin of the need to control is always based on fear. This fear insists that I will miss opportunities, that there won't be enough, that things won't work out in my favor, or that something will be lost. All of these fears amount to one thing: death.

My relationship with death has been one of avoidance, terror, and pain. Having not experienced it yet in relationships with loved ones, it feels even more threatening and ominous. The more I cherish my own precious life, the more I distance myself from the thought of death.

Between my need to control to avoid loss and my need to thrive in exuberance in order to defy death, I have been building myself up and up, only to find myself wielding a sledgehammer towards this false foundation.

The journey of encountering humility and undergoing the process of surrender is a life-long endeavor; we can never expect it to be complete. It is the understanding of ourselves as continually in progress and the knowing that we are perfect even in our imperfections that will give us relief and satisfaction. True accomplishment lies not in just reaching the top of the mountain, but in knowing that we will always tie our boots back up for the next adventure.

That said, our ambitions and aspirations are beautiful things. While a flower in bloom seems entirely beautiful in the present, it is both growing roots into the earth and shooting skywards all at once. Steadfast in its solidity, still a tree does not stop yearning to touch the sky. Likewise, our dreams will always follow and remember us. Beckoning for us to heed them, they will haunt us even if we attempt to neglect them.

For me, a huge transition occurred when I realized this distinction. It was crucial to identify *what* I wanted in life, but just as critical to surrender to the process of *how* it would manifest. Once you know what you want, setting the intention and launching it is the first step. Most of us tend to then take that same self-agency and determine each of the following steps too, all the way until gaining the outcome we desire. But often, what we think is the best way is in fact so limited. When we become more receptive and allow for different options and perspectives to come our way, we can realize more good happening than we ever deemed possible. We can bring all the ingredients to the table, but often our intuition knows more than we do...

And a large dollop of trust goes a long way.

Lesson 4 – Ask yourself: Have I Connected with Love Today?

Years ago, in a similar moment of true surrender, I lay sobbing on a bed, experiencing the soft subdued elation of true peace that comes from letting go. Recently getting over a break up, I stopped chasing my attachment to a need for validation and love from a certain source, and connected to the larger Source; the one filled with love that was flowing from a deep fountain within me.

It was in that moment that I wrote this piece:

The instant I get out of my own way,
let go,
and forgive others
and even myself,
all the judgments, anger, accusations, and assumptions melt.

I don't have to prove myself anymore.
I don't have to defend myself anymore.

My castle opens its door into a gentle garden overflowing with green,
and I experience the Divinity
which has always been a part of me.

I remember I'm here to be a servant of love,
and a vessel for its manifestation.

And still I cry,
because we have union
and we have separation,
and we are small and embodied,
and that hurts.

So everyday, I will ask myself:

"Have you connected with love today?"
Because- what else matters more?
What else should shape our days and our dreaming?
Our dealings and our desires?
What else should emanate, radiate, expand inside us?

...Give birth to love today.
Choose it. Let it choose you.

All you have to do is open your heart and say "yes".

About the Author

Jeanine Nicole is a workshop facilitator, life coach, writer, and yoga instructor who lives in New York City. Jeanine combines her compassionate sensitivity, open-minded curiosity, and love of deep personal transformation in her writings and life. A former social worker and educator with a passion for global activism and community service, she believes that much lasting change in our world begins from the inside out.

She is passionate about poetry, creative expression, aligning her activities with her interests, and helping others to similarly follow their bliss.

http://www.beginwithin18.com/

THE JOURNEY OF THE HEART

Dellaina Almora

~Love knows no bounds, and exceeds time and space~

A shudder of fear ran through her body. Dana began to shake. 'I can't speak to you now,' she said and hastily clicked down the phone. What had come over her? With tears running down her cheeks, she was at a loss to understand her reactions to his words. Stumbling outside into the light of the full moon, she laid on the grass, calling to the heavens to help her release the pain, which was increasing in her heart and pulsating through every part of her body.

It was a holiday weekend away with her friends on a country retreat. Enjoying the solitude, looking forward to her love's return from his six-week stay at sea. Whetu would return home for two months before embarking on a Polynesian waka (canoe) voyage across the Pacific. When the call came, he was to leave earlier than expected, giving the lovers only a short time together between each journey.

Never before had Dana felt such excruciating pain. It felt as if her own soul was being torn away. Eventually, exhausted and falling into a partial dream state, a vision became clear.

She was now in the North Americas, hundreds of years earlier observing and then experiencing her self at dawn, in the cool desert canyon. At the same time, she could feel the fresh damp grass under her naked body as the moon lit up the sleeping country garden. She watched two Indians very much in love, looking deeply into each other's eyes.

No words were spoken, yet she could feel his fate. Her love was determined, for this was the journey of the warrior; his honor depended on it. He must follow the ancient traditions of his ancestors. As the horses' flowing mane sailed upwards into the breeze, she watched him hold out his warrior staff in farewell salute. Galloping away at great speed, his silhouette shrunk into obscurity. Onwards to his vision quest, his fate was now sealed.

Dana knew it would be the last time she would see him alive. Unable to share this knowing, or distract him from his journey, she stood in numbed silence. Although the sun was now rising and the light was cascading into beautiful colors, the canyon might as well have been shrouded with thunder clouds and shadow. For her the desert now felt threatening and unforgiving.

Stirring deep within her heart, she was reminded of their love and of trusting their soul's journey. This gave her courage; death would not separate them.

The love and wisdom in that moment became stronger than the grief and fear that continued to shudder through her in waves. She stood for hours… or was it days? Finally, someone from the village found her sobbing, and carried her home to the safety of the clan.

A few days later while tending the village fire, sudden pain piercing through her like a knife, she collapsed to the ground. Dana knew his soul had departed and that she must go to him. She rode off into the night, adrenalin pumping through her body. It was two days or more, guided by her heart, before she found where her love laid.

At last, with his loyal horse close by, there he was with an arrow in his eye and a tomahawk in his chest. She laid beside him weeping uncontrollably for days.

Eerie shadows now cast about her as she awoke to the bright light of the moon back in the present moment, disoriented and confused. What did this mean? What was the message from beyond the grave and a life past? There were many more questions, but no answers were forthcoming.

Returning home after the retreat in the country, she lit a candle and breathed deeply into her nightly meditation. A Maori elder she had known for many years appeared in spirit form. He was a trained shaman from the ancient lore of the land. His totem animal was the hawk, and it often appeared when she thought of him.

Now he was very agitated and demanded that she write down an important message. The words flowed onto her pad, and in a trance-like state, two pages were soon filled.

The next day the news came that the elder had died!

After reading his message, Dana realized the previous night's visit was from his departing spirit, come to confess and ask for forgiveness. Only then would he be free from the guilt and resentments of the past and released from the bounds of the earthly plain.

The month before, Dana had taken Whetu to meet this very sick elder. They travelled many hours to take healing to him, sadly feeling this may be their last meeting.

Whetu was still working at sea; when they had their daily conversation Dana told him the news. He was silent for a moment and then said that on that day, a hawk had flown and landed on the ship that he was working on. It was very unusual and he had never seen one in all the years at sea before.

Had the elder visited Whetu as well? Did he have a message to pass before his soul took its final flight home?

As the weeks went by, more visions came to Dana in many stages, revealing the names of the Indians from her first vision. Many more insights came clear about their influence in her life with Whetu now. With each memory of that past lifetime, came release and the clearing of a deep healing process. Each vision showed how these experiences of the past had been re-created in this lifetime, causing pain in their separate journeys.

Whetu was just about to go on another major journey, which had not been taken for hundreds of years by his ancestors: to sail across the Pacific on a Polynesian Waka. The purpose: to highlight the plight of the world's oceans and to adopt a more sustainable and healthy way of living.

When Whetu returned from the ship, Dana took the pad with the elder's words and read it out. It was addressed to him.

"My dear beloved brother of the four winds, as I draw my last breath and in the twilight moments between the worlds, all has become clear to me. Our meeting has greater significance to us than I could have realized, while in my sick and mallard state. I was unable to see the gift that was brought before me.

I reach out to you now and ask for love and forgiveness, for it was me that ended your life on that vision quest. I was your brother, Sun Eagle.

Matters of the human heart and their fragilities are the greatest test of a man's faith. Please take 'Hine Moana' on your voyage as a symbol of love, healing, and togetherness, so that we can all be joined once more in the love that we shared in the clan.

I love you my brother, I will be watching over you with safe passage and healing light. My journey in this world is no more; I am part of the wind, the sky, and the stars.

Blessings to you my brother, your friend and guide now in spirit. My love of two moons once divided us and now unites us."

As Whetu read the words, tears began to fall, his heart knowing the truth; the healing was taking place deep within his own heart and soul. It was Sun Eagle that killed Lightning Stallion (now Whetu) on that vision quest a life time before. Whetu put *Hine Moana* around his neck where she has remained. The healing path was calling.

Had it already began a very long time ago?

A few years prior, the elder had gifted Dana a beautiful green stone – Pounamu named *Hine Moana* (maiden of the ocean) – as a mark of appreciation and respect for her conservation work for the oceans. Hine Moana is a powerful taonga (sacred treasure). She had worn it proudly, only on special ceremonial occasions.

As the time drew near for his waka journey, the fear returned from deep inside her. Was this now another opportunity for his soul to complete the vision quest that had been started a lifetime before?

Dana feared he may never return and she could not bear losing him again. The feelings were so real, the fear so raw, that the mind battled with the seemingly absurd and the soul called out in desperation.

Were these messages from the elder the warning? Or was the Indian woman giving her a premonition, this time to stop him from going? Was it now time to finish what had begun all those years ago?

Life suddenly took another twist in the road. A call came to say Dana's father was gravely ill. They were again to be separated; two individual journeys two individual quests.

There was to be no contact while he travelled across the ocean on the waka and she was guided by spirit to remember the ways of old. Communication had to come through prayer, mediation, and telepathy. This, she did day and night.

Reaching his hospital bed, Dana made the journey back to her father's side. Having had major surgery, she visited him daily but was deeply troubled.

A month later, while walking the windy cliff of her beautiful island, a message finally came from her beloved, Whetu, thousands of miles away. Now ashore in North America, having reached the first destination, there were to be three more weeks of sailing before completing the journey. Although ecstatic to hear his voice at last, her spirit was waning and she ached to see him. Every hour felt like a week; the nights were long and dark.

Days later within the stark corridor of the hospital ward, a call came through. "I am getting off the waka. I know you are struggling, I want to help, and I would like to come to you now."

His love and sincerity ran deep.

How could she agree? The vision quest was incomplete. He had not made it last time, so allowing him to abandon the cause at this late stage felt so wrong – the message from the elder and the beautiful souls that spoke from beyond the veils.

She agonized, praying for guidance, because this could not just be about her human needs, but their soul's great journey.

Suddenly, like a flash of lightning, all became clear.

The initiation or vision quest, even back then, was for Lightening Stallion to listen to his heart, despite the consequences. Instead he followed the traditions of his people and the ancestors. For going against the elders and clan's traditions was not ever a pathway to consider.

Even though Whetu's waka journey was for a cause, of healing the oceans, humanity, and the earth, for him the real vision quest was to choose the heart journey over the waka one. He had not done this as Lightening Stallion in the last vision quest. It was a similar choice but with a different time, place, cause, fleet, and crew.

There was no failing by not completing the waka voyage. Following his heart's calling was the vision quest! To go to his loved ones side. This knowing came with great inspiration and power; the feeling for them both surged like an exploding star.

The soul's voice was finally heard; he made the voyage across the world to her side.

At last, reunited in this truth, their hearts were at peace and their souls were free. The long journeys were complete.

Two moons and Lightning Stallion were also free to journey home to their own world.

His horse moved swiftly through the desert sand as the rising sun-light filled their hearts with love and joy. The light returned; free to go on to the soul's home now.

The vision quest: Complete.

About the Author

Dellaina is a visionary therapist and channel for Almora. Almora is an expanded group consciousness that identifies with the powerful life force of our sun, now working from spirit to assist humanity in the great changes occurring on our planet.

Originally, Dellaina comes from an Island called Jersey off the coast of France. After travelling extensively around the world, she made her home in Christchurch, New Zealand.

As well as the channel for Almora, Dellaina draws from a wide range of skills, including divination, astrology, shamanism, and past life therapy.

"My passion is working with people finding their inner power of creation, leading to the most, expanded, loving, abundant and adventurous life possible. I am also very interested in soulful relationships, which is becoming an increasing focus of our work."

She runs a busy practice with her partner, Ihaia, in Christchurch, also facilitating retreats, courses and workshops around the globe.

http://www.almora.co.nz

THE FINE PRINT

Maureen (Moe) Wood

Being an earth person is hard. I bet a lot of people wish leaving the birth canal was optional!

For a long time I thought my soul must have miscalculated its trajectory. I was supposed to show up on the *enlightened earth*. It's a place full of Empaths and people who use telepathy and emotional communication. It's awesome because nothing can be misunderstood when thoughts are conveyed as pure energy. On enlightened earth people inspire others; they are constantly saying, "Atta girl and atta boy" to each other! The enlightened earth people are passionate, loving, and kind. They pursue wisdom, not ownership. Borders and lines of demarcation don't exist. Everything you need to learn can be learned the enlightened way.

I was supposed to go there. Something obviously went side-ways.

Those of us who have been given a glimpse of what enlightened earth is like are trying hard to spread the message! In the meantime we have a human experience and learn the *human* way, at least until the Universe smacks us so hard we can't pretend to be *just* human anymore.

When I arrived, I realized I was stuck in a body that stopped me from doing what I knew was possible. I couldn't think of someone and suddenly be with them. I couldn't send a mental thought to someone and have it received. I hated using spoken communication because everything was always getting screwed up! People heard what they *thought* I said, not what I *actually* said.

The things I could see with my human eyes were a fraction of what I knew existed. I didn't have anybody to talk to about my spiritual and mystical experiences. There were no books to read and no computers back then to Google metaphysics. Being a metaphysician and Sensitive was not considered a good thing when I was a kid; I was called a freak so often I started to believe it and I shut down.

It got to the point where wanting to feel normal and included became the most important thing and I was willing to pay a price, ignoring who I really was.

Being an Empath in the teenage years was like having hormones on crack. I needed the turbulence to stop and I tried to feel included by doing some stupid stuff. If being mean and gossiping and discovering that acting tough was going to help me feel ordinary, I was in. The fact that beer helped me discover I could be funny was a bonus. Boys were a nice distraction too; paying attention to them was fun and much more acceptable than talking to dead people.

Whatever I needed to do, however fake I had to be, if it meant feeling included I was on board. I was happy to lower my energy to match my surroundings if it meant I didn't feel like an outcast.

Choosing between being myself and belonging was cruel. Surely the Universe had shredded my contract and stuck me with someone else's. I existed within that conundrum until the day my soul became louder than my desire to fit in.

It was the most pivotal day of my life.

I was nineteen and was walking from school to my friend's house one day. I walked past a construction project where dozens of guys were working. I walked past them and right after that I saw a man walking toward me and my intuitive radar went off the charts. Something was wrong.

I wondered if I felt uncomfortable because his skin color was different than mine. I'd been raised in an area where people were quick to form judgments about people who were different. I'd sworn I'd never do that and so I told myself to ignore my intuition in case I was judging and smiled at him as he crossed to my side of the sidewalk. After all, his outer behavior seemed normal enough. And I was committed to proving I didn't judge based on outer appearance.

When he was face to face with me he said, "Do you have a smoke?"

I said, "No. I don't smoke.".

"OK," he said and walked past me.

Suddenly he grabbed me from behind, one hand over my mouth and the other at my back, pushing me across the street. I couldn't get traction because the street was slippery.

"Thank God for those guys down the street," I thought. "I have to hang on for a couple seconds and they will come!"

I was taken to an abandoned garage. The attacker pushed me against a wall and started tearing my clothes. I heard a nonphysical voice say, "Stay on your feet. Lean against the wall!"

I was screaming inside my head, but my vocal cords were frozen. I got more instructions: "Push him here, elbow him there, avoid eye contact."

After a few minutes of struggling I was getting tired. He was getting more aggressive and I didn't know how much longer I could stay on my feet.

I heard a sound. It seemed like something had fallen on top of the garage. Then it happened again, this time like something had broken as it landed. The rapist heard it too. He put his hand over my mouth to keep me quiet. There was another clunk, then another. The rapist ran out the door threatening to find me if I told anyone. I was shaking and trying to wrap my head around what had happened.

I picked up my things, ran to my friend's house, and she called 911.

Eventually I recovered from the trauma and went through the police investigation, but once that was over I had time to think about what the police told me after they had gone to the scene to investigate.

After they'd interviewed me on the day of the attack, they went to the abandoned garage. They realized it was semi-detached from a house built into the hillside. This wasn't obvious from the street. That explained why noises made in the house could be heard in the garage.

When they interviewed the homeowner he was distraught, not only because a girl had been attacked in his garage, but also because he had never come home during the day before until *that* day.

The reason he'd come home was because he was giving an afternoon presentation at work and had gotten to the office before realizing what he needed had been left at home. The police said it rattled him pretty bad. He'd helped save a girl from a much worse attack because he happened to forget something that day and happened to come home exactly in time to scare the rapist.

The police interviewed the construction crew too. They said they saw it happen, but thought they were seeing a lovers' quarrel. They didn't want to interfere.

Really? A man crosses the road and grabs a girl, forcing her off the street is a lovers' quarrel? To what rational person does that sound like anything other than what it is? Once I got over my anger about that, I saw it from the spiritual perspective.

Because they *didn't* rescue me, I found myself in a situation where I could once again hear the voices of my nonphysical family. I was also reminded that my instincts are more accurate than what any outer circumstances might indicate.

It may have taken a lot longer for me to embrace my uniqueness if that event hadn't happened.

That day I was reminded of these truths: my intuition is right, every time. It is my God-given guidance system. I have access to a nonphysical support system.

We all do.

We are entangled for group and individual lessons. We experience them as human beings but the lessons are for the soul. When someone hurts us, there is an energy exchange that teaches us something. The encounter may remind us of something or reflect to us how far we've come. We are *progress indicators* to one other.

I had to be shocked into understanding my uniqueness was not a mistake! I had to be traumatized into listening to my intuition and remembering my soul mattered. I had to be put in harm's way before I paid attention to the nonphysical support system I had ignored for years.

The story of my personal wakeup call illustrates what is happening with humanity as a whole. The Universe is screaming for humanity to wake up. Many of us, though not enough, have.

What if masses of people could be reminded of their soul's unique vibration through stories and lectures and spontaneous soul memories instead of violence and natural disasters? What if they could be stirred into awakening and remembering in an enlightened way? What if Earth could retain all her physical beauty but the Sun became brighter, the wind freer, the water more clear, and the hearts of humanity held no sadness or pain? Would you want to live there?

If enough of us do decide to think our way into enlightened earth, it will be done.

We – the Earth people here now – can call forth enlightened earth by thinking it into the physical dimension. This is not the business of the left-brain intellect. Enlightened earth is the work of the heart. Emotional (heart generated) communication *cannot* be misinterpreted on the energetic realm. We can manifest Earth's enlightened equivalent by believing we can. We do not need more wakeup calls!

Let's be the generation that believes in enlightened earth in great enough numbers to get the job done. We'll continue to be reflections to one another, but the reflections will be so much brighter!

When I got here I was disappointed. I remembered who I was but Earth wasn't like she was supposed to be. Then I tried to forget who I was to better match my surroundings. I finally realized that my biggest contribution might be found in my differences.

One of those differences is my awareness of the nonphysical dimensions. Enlightened earth does exist there. It's being made ready now. We can bring it into tangible reality. We can do it because we believe we can! Picture it in your minds' eye. Feel the thought travel through your heart. Send the image forth to the Universe as heart-waves and it shall be done!

Maybe I was upset when I got here because I read the fine print too fast.

Maybe our contracts didn't say, "You will go to the enlightened earth." Maybe they said, "You will go to enlighten the earth."

About the Author

Maureen Wood (Moe) has been writing passionately since fifth grade when her Aunt who was colleagues with Oxford professor P.J. Potts asked him to critique one of her non-fiction pieces. His favorable analysis of her writing at such a young age is something for which Moe remains grateful. Moe authors a blog titled *Metaphysics for Earth People*, hosts spiritual/mediumship development groups and is a member of the Northwest Mediumship Association. She studies soul-connections, unscrambling and explaining in layman's terms how human experiences affect one's soul-evolution and vice-versa.

Moe is a dimensional interpreter. She communicates with caring beings in other dimensions and delivers their messages to humans. In addition to being a medium and intuitive she is a conduit for a multitude of quantum frequencies used for healing. She is particularly adept at working with physical illness and injury.

http://www.twinflames.com

AN AMERICAN GIRL IN PARIS

Mary Knebel

I would venture to say that most people on the planet have heard of the Eiffel Tower or have seen a picture of it. Many lucky people have even travelled to Paris at some point in their lives to see it in person. I had the good fortune of actually living in Paris for two years as a young woman fresh out of college, and seeing the Eiffel Tower (and Notre Dame) on a daily basis. For me it was literally a dream come true. More importantly, what I learned from that experience has become a sort of guide for me in showing me how to make my dreams come true.

And I hope it will do the same for you!

As a little girl, I always had an active imagination and big dreams. Quite simply, I wanted to grow up, move to France, and become fluent in French. Never mind that I had never been to France, had absolutely no idea how I was going to make it happen, and had no clue of why I wanted to make this happen so badly in the first place. I was just a little girl dreaming about the future, as we all do.

French was a mandatory subject from kindergarten until fifth grade at school, and during those classes the language had always just made sense to me. As I continued throughout my childhood and took my language classes every year, I also continued imagining that someday I would live in Paris and would be able to speak the language effortlessly. I translated songs that came on the radio, and even had my mom subscribe me to a magazine that was entirely in French, despite the fact that I could barely understand what it said. At a certain point I remember acting act out skits with friends from school, in which we pretended we were very sophisticated and living in France. We would utter a lot of *bonjour* and *oui, oui*!

Fast forward to the time when I was a senior in college: Everyone was applying for post-graduation jobs in major cities like Atlanta, San Francisco, New York, and Washington, DC, but all I could think of was living and working in France! (During my junior year, I had spent a semester studying near the French Riviera and had decided it was definitely the place for me.) Like everyone else I applied to some of the big-name consulting firms, and even secured a few interviews, but nothing really stuck. If truth be told, all I wanted to do was travel back to France, have some sort of grand adventure, and learn how to really speak the language once and for all. I told myself I would stay for six months, explore Europe a bit, and then return home to the US to begin my post-college life in the real world.

I did end up living there (Paris specifically) for two years right after college. Once I arrived, through a series of coincidences, I found a job as a translator in a large international law firm, eventually found an adorable studio apartment on the Ile St. Louis (the smaller of the two islands in the Seine), made the right connections with people who could help me on my path, and finally became fluent! To be honest, once I made the decision that I was going to make this happen, things pretty much fell into place for me and unfolded as if by cue. It wasn't necessarily easy, and required a lot of courage, faith, and action on my part. But those two years spent in Paris were certainly two of the best years of my life.

While there, I spent hours upon hours walking the streets of Paris, soaking up the culture and the language, not to mention eating in café after café, day after day. I felt a freedom I had never felt before, and for those two years I really felt like I had come home. Something had been calling to me all those years as a little girl, and I had finally found it. I felt alive, on-purpose, and truly connected to myself, life, and the world as a whole.

I've now been back in the US for several years, and with some perspective I can see it wasn't just luck or coincidence that was involved in my adventure. To me, my journey represents a true love for self and a *oneness* with the Universe at its very core. That is, when you uncover a dream or passion and believe in yourself no matter what, the way to accomplish it will be unveiled to you and everything will unfold as it needs to. I don't think there's any greater act of self-love than opening up to your greatest desires and committing to bring them forward into reality, no matter what it takes.

When I was a young twenty-two year-old heading out on the international flight overseas, with nothing more than two large suitcases stuffed completely full, I believed in myself and had absolute faith that what I wanted was possible. No one was going to stop me from making my dream to live in France come true. I had some money to get me started and enough desire to carry me forward. Besides, I was twenty-two!

What did I know?

To be frank, I do think I had youth and naivety on my side and hadn't yet been exposed to some of the harsh realities of the real world. However, I don't think one should underestimate the power of believing in yourself. It never occurred to me that I wouldn't find an affordable (and chic!) place to live, a job to pay the bills, or people to guide me on my path and socialize with.

This is so important in making big dreams come true in our lives. Ultimately, if you don't believe deep down that you can make something happen, you won't take the necessary actions to help you succeed. Even if you can't predict how your dream is going to unfold, it is vital that on some level you have enough belief in yourself to know that you will eventually make your wildest dreams come true. Sometimes it's just an intense desire that precedes everything else that gets you to take action. But there always has to be something inside you that believes it's worthwhile to go for what you want and that there will be a reward at the end of the journey. Otherwise, all the excuses in the world will rise to the surface to stop you from moving forward.

Another lesson I learned is that you won't always be able to see the entire path to making your dreams come true laid out before you. Often, when you're inspired to accomplish something big, you're not given the whole picture at one time. Instead, you're just given the next step in front of you. Once you take that step, you'll be shown the step that follows. It's a one-step-at-a-time process. To start, though, you must take the step that's directly in front of you (and sometimes that step is really scary!). The truth is: When I moved to Paris, I didn't have a clue how anything would turn out. I didn't know where I would live, or work, or if I would even be able to fully understand the language. However, I just kept moving and didn't look back.

I recently learned from a mentor of mine that everything you want is just on the other side of that fear that is preventing you from taking that next step in front of you. Think about that for a second.

Everything you want is waiting for you.

But it's right outside that fear or obstacle that seems so big and insurmountable right now. Which means you better get moving! Fear can sometimes seem downright debilitating, however if you remind yourself that your dream is there on the other side of it, waiting for you, you will have that extra push needed to get through the fear. Furthermore, the faster you move through fear, the faster it is over and done with!

Also vitally important in making your dreams come true is visualization, or really seeing and stepping into your dreams as if they've already come true. As a little girl I didn't realize what I was doing. However, years later when I actually found myself living in the City of Lights, I reflected back to the times when I acted out skits as if I was living in France and was amazed at how similarly my real life reflected what I was make-believing back then (down to the type of job I had and the French family I became close with). Without even knowing it, I had been using the powers of creative visualization and really stepping into my dream as if it were already a reality. Most people have heard of the powers of visualization, but this is a real-life example that shows how vividly it can turn out.

Finally, know that if you desire something strongly enough, it will eventually find you, even if there are a few bumps in the road. I didn't mention it earlier, but when I was a freshman in college, I tested out of the first few years of college French and was placed in a much higher level French course. Unfortunately, I did horribly in the class, didn't really understand much at all that the professor was saying, and ended up dropping French entirely from my major. At that point I was completely turned off by the language, and decided to forget about France all together. Besides, I was in college and had parties to attend!

This should have been the end of my fascination with France, except that two years later practically all of my friends were planning on spending a semester studying abroad. I knew that if I didn't go I would be left behind in the States and would have to make all new friends, which didn't appeal to me. At all. I quickly enrolled in a French course, and was accepted in the same study abroad program as all my friends.

I spent a semester abroad in the south of France in an adorable little town called Aix-en-Provence, and my dreams of living in France were back on track. Even though I had gotten in my own way, there was a bigger picture that eventually pulled me back to my original desire. The same thing will happen to you. If you want something badly enough and truly believe it is meant for you, you can rest assured knowing that life and the Universe always have your back, and that they will give you more and more opportunities until you finally get it right!

These days I'm working on manifesting different dreams, but I still try to get back to Paris every year or two. While I'm there, I always remind myself of what I learned during my grand adventure overseas: Anything is possible as long as you know what it is that will really excite you and light you up. Then, believe in yourself knowing deep down you can make it happen, imagine yourself in that reality as often as possible, and take inspired action as it comes to you, step by step.

Big dreams can still be really daunting, but the way through that fear is to just keep moving forward and taking action. One day you will turn around and realize you've accomplished your dreams and are actually living right in the middle of them! By then most of us have already moved on to the next big vision we want to create, so always remember to stop for a bit and enjoy what you've created as much as you can.

About the Author

Mary Knebel is a client attraction and prosperity coach who is passionate about helping others make their wildest dreams come true. She believes that everyone has their own special *wildest dream* that they can bring to reality, and works with spiritual and heart-centered individuals to help them do just that.

Her programs help budding entrepreneurs who crave the freedom lifestyle to unearth their authentic purpose, attract their ideal clients, increase their income, and ultimately create the life of their dreams.

She is an avid traveler and loves the idea of being able to run her business from anywhere in the world.

http://www.attractingyouridealclients.com

LOVE DELIVERS HOPE

Sarah Centrella

It's funny how the meaning of true love can change over time. How you can go through your entire life believing you understand what it encompasses and what it means to you. What categories of love different people in your life fall into, and then one day something happens to turn all your ideas upside down.

That's what happened to me.

I had married my *one true love* in 2000, who was my high school sweetheart. I felt I knew exactly what love was, how it felt, and what it stood for.

That was until September of 2008. It was just three months after my identical twin girls turned a year old that I discovered my husband was having an affair. To say it came as a shock is beyond an understatement. I had no clue. We had just downsized our life so we could afford to become a family of five once the twins arrived. I had been through hell already the previous two years; losing our home to foreclosure, having our family car repossessed, being forced into bankruptcy with excessive medical bills from the twins, and losing a baby. It was a seemingly never-ending cycle of darkness and bad luck, which culminated on that September day.

The day I found out, I had nothing. No access to bank accounts, not five dollars to my name. The rent and utilities were past due and I was out of formula and diapers for the babies. My husband had been our only source of income, and when he left so did the ability to feed and take care of my family.

That night amid the devastation and my inability to inhabit my body or feel reality, I remember my girlfriend walking through the front door. I don't remember what was said. But what I do remember were her arms overflowing with Costco boxed diapers, cans of formula, food, and enough cash to keep the water and lights on. I think I was lying on the floor sobbing; I honestly don't remember.

That moment was the defining moment of my life. It was the moment that has driven my relentless pursuit. It was the moment I hustle and grind for; the reason I get up when the floor looks like such a damn good alternative; the reason I *stand*. That was the moment I learned that true love can include more than just romantic love. That when someone honestly loves you, they will go the distance for you. They will have your back in any situation. They will stand by your side no matter what, through thick and thin.

I knew on that day that I had only one choice: survival. I had no idea how I could possibly do it on my own with no job, no income, no savings, no bank account or credit. I knew we couldn't stay in our current home without an income, but, I had no idea how to get another place to live. It seemed beyond hopeless. It felt like I was being asked to move a mountain when I wasn't even capable of climbing it. The only thing I was sure of was I'd do whatever it took to take care of my three babies. I'd work any job, live anywhere, do whatever I had to, to insure they would always be with me and taken care of.

So I started over at the very bottom with nothing more than determination and a dream for a better life; one I could control and envision.

Within a week of him leaving, I sold everything we owned that I could fetch ten dollars for, wedding rings included. Everything I'd spent a lifetime acquiring… sold to the first Craigslist caller. I raised enough funds to move us from our home to a tiny two-bedroom apartment. I searched day and night for a job, keeping the fact that I was now a single mom of three young children, a secret as long as possible. Finally, I got a position with a salary big enough to cover rent, daycare, and car payments, nothing more. But I was happy and proud to have it and believed it would get better.

This was the start to my new life. I just *knew* it. I wanted a better life for my children than I had been able to give them in the past, one better than what I had known as a child. I looked at them and realized that they were the embodiment of unconditional, pure love. They loved me the same every day, even on the really bad ones; they gave me what a man never could. Complete, honest, unadulterated love. I wanted to make them proud and give them reason to always believe in themselves and in me.

So I began to dream.

I dusted off an old vision board I had created almost two years prior, after I'd first seen Oprah's show on *The Secret*, and took it to my new office. On it, pictures of Time Square in New York City, The Las Vegas strip (The Paris Hotel), a tropical island, the Hollywood sign, designer stilettos, and a Mercedes Benz. Everything on my board seemed so ridiculously out of the question at the time, it was almost embarrassing. But it made me happy to look at my pictures all day and imagine what life would be like if I was experiencing all those amazing things.

A year passed and I was offered a sales job with another software company. Three months into my new position and the CEO came to me and gave me that chance. He offered me the opportunity to launch a brand new division of the company and be a director/vice president.

I loved my new job. I worked hard, day and night, and was driven; motivated in a way I had never been before. I woke up one day and realized that I was happy. The kids and I were alive and surviving. Even more so, we were starting to thrive.

Then one day, as I frantically packed my desk making sure I had everything for my trip to New York in the morning, I paused and looked at my vision board. I got instant chills and tears filled my eyes when I noticed the picture of the Hollywood sign, which I had seen the day before on a business trip to Los Angeles. Then I saw the photo of Time Square right in the center, the biggest picture on the board. Below the picture I had written in big capital letters "NYC BABY!!!" almost two years before... back when I was still married, broke, and depressed. I looked down at the e-ticket to JFK in my hand and tears welled up in my eyes.

This was the first time I realized I could create the life I wanted; that I *already had*.

Last summer, due to flooding, one of our industry trade-shows was moved last minute from Nashville, Tennessee, to Las Vegas, Nevada. I was looking forward to the trip since I was pretty sure I was the only adult on the West Coast who had never been there. It was a fun, long, hot exhausting week, and I was glad to be on the plane home. When I got back to the office and saw the picture on my vision board, I got chills. It took me about two hours to notice the center of the picture, which was the Paris Hotel. I had stayed at the Paris Hotel all week. I hadn't booked the reservation! It was all done for me without my input through my work travel agent.

The Law of Attraction was really starting to freak me out. That was when it clicked that this wasn't a vision board per se; it was a *future board*! Since that moment on, I began to be very aware of my thoughts, feelings, words, and actions. I began paying close attention to my vision board and realized I had manifested more than I even realized.

Since then, I've stayed in luxury hotels and eaten at five-star restaurants. I've flown first class and had limos and drivers take me wherever I needed to go. I've watched a New York Knicks game from the official Knicks team sky box with Knicks coaches and executives. I've watched my son meet NBA players while sitting on the NBA bench post game. I've, walked on the NFL Baltimore Ravens field, and watched the team warm-up with my son before a game. I've surfed in Hawaii behind my son who got up his first try! I've fallen asleep under a panoramic view of the Empire State Building, in my two bedroom penthouse suite. I've lived so many *pinch me moments*. Did I mention that I did all of this without spending a dime of my own money... in just eighteen months? Now... do you believe that *anything* is possible? Do you believe in magic?

I say all of this not to brag or boast; I say it to *inspire* you. Realize that you are the only person/thing (not money, not circumstances, not other people in your life) that stands in the way of what is possible for you. You don't need to be rich to live the life of your dreams. All you need is the ability to define your dreams, be willing to work toward them, believe in magic, and then watch your life change and unfold.

This year I made a *new* vision board. I dreamed even bigger this time and I've been watching those dreams manifest as well. But all of this wasn't by luck or chance. It was by design and purposeful intention. It was a conscious effort to transform a tragedy into my triumph. It was me looking for the *reason* behind what had happened to me, and then learning how to control my future outcomes. .

Learning how to bring blessings where there used to be only curses. I look at my life today and all I can think, is how blessed I am. How grateful I am for all the trials and obstacles I have faced, they truly have made me stronger. They have taught me to trust and believe that everything which comes into my life really does have a purpose. It's my choice how I deal with it; whether I let it devour me or chose to rise above it.

Now I know that love goes beyond a broken heart. That the human spirit is capable of deep, connected love on multiple fronts. And that in life there is *not* just one person we are meant to love, but many. Now I know that loving someone, even a friend, can provide them hope and motivation that neither of you might recognize until much later. Giving love, unconditional love, to the people in our lives helps them take on challenges and gives them the strength they need to *stand*. I believe in the magic of love to give hope and strength where none existed before.

About the Author

Sarah Centrella is the author of the personal memoir *Thoughts. Stories. Life.*, based loosely on her motivational blog of the same name. She writes about her personal experience of going from *nothin' to somethin'* and reinventing her life.

Her short stories are award winning, and Marco Polo Literary Magazine chose her as one of their top 100 writers of 2012. She now consults clients individually as a life coach with practice areas specializing in the Law of Attraction and athletic life coaching. She is also a motivational speaker, sharing her passion for helping others achieve their goals, dreams and the life they envision.

Sarah is a single mother of three small children, who lives and works in Seattle, WA, as the director of business development for a consulting company. She is passionate about sharing her story to motivate and inspire others around the world.

http://www.sarahcentrella.com

SHARE YOUR STORY AND JOIN THE COMMUNITY

Have a Story to Share?

Everyone has a story, including you! With several *Adventures in Manifesting* titles in production each year, we are constantly looking for more journeys to share. Ask yourself, *what story of mine could change someone's life?*

Whether you have a story to tell or lesson to teach, we're listening. Share yours and get the guide to writing and submitting your chapter here:

www.AdventuresInManifesting.org

The stories we keep an eye out for are any that has to do with manifesting (success, spirituality, health, happiness, wealth, love prosperity, inner guidance, achieving dreams, overcoming obstacles, etc.).

If chosen as a top submission, we will get in touch directly to invite you to be a part of one of our next *Adventures in Manifesting* titles.

Looking for Guidance?

AdventuresInManifesting.org is also a place to freely join a course & community with lessons and action guides for manifesting.

By training you to develop rituals for success and creating the space to get the energy flowing, it will enable you to focus on your intentions from the purest place possible.

www.AdventuresInManifesting.org

Join now to surround yourself with some incredible individuals. It truly is a place of joyful intention marked with the loving energy of gratitude and appreciation.

Feeling Inspired?

We always love to hear how our readers were touched, inspired or changed by the stories shared. If you'd like to share your experience, then you guessed it, hop on over to the AdventuresInManifesting.org home page to let us know!

MORE ADVENTURES IN MANIFESTING TITLES

--iBooks and Kindle--

All Älska titles can be found through the www.AdventuresInManifesting.org portal or requested from your local bookstore (and found through online bookstores as well).

<u>Books</u>

Adventures in Manifesting: Success and Spirituality

Adventures in Manifesting: Health and Happiness

Adventures in Manifesting: Passion and Purpose

Adventures in Manifesting: Healing from Within

Adventures in Manifesting: Love and Oneness

<u>The Kindle and iBooks</u>

Each of the Adventures in Manifesting titles above can also be purchased via the Amazon Kindle or iTunes iBook formats via AdventuresInManifesting.org.

SHARE WITH LOVE

Is someone you know on the deep and profound journey within? If so, be sure to share with them the entire book or specific stories you intuitively felt would resonate with them.

The meaning of Älska is 'to Love' (it's a Swedish Verb!)

The *chapters* were written with Love.

The *book* was published with Love.

And now it's up to you to *share* with Love.

From the bottom of our hearts and deepest depths of our soul, thank you, thank you, thank you.

With Love & Gratitude,

Älska

http://www.AlskaPublishing.com